Utilitarianism

Utilitarianism

John Stuart Mill

Edited by Andrew Bailey

This edition is adapted from
The Broadview Anthology of Social and Political Thought;

General Editors:

Andrew Bailey
Samantha Brennan
Will Kymlicka
Jacob Levy
Alex Sager
Clark Wolf

broadview press

BROADVIEW PRESS – www.broadviewpress.com
Peterborough, Ontario, Canada

Founded in 1985, Broadview Press remains a wholly independent publishing house. Broadview's focus is on academic publishing; our titles are accessible to university and college students as well as scholars and general readers. With over 600 titles in print, Broadview has become a leading international publisher in the humanities, with world-wide distribution. Broadview is committed to environmentally responsible publishing and fair business practices.

The interior of this book is printed
on 100% recycled paper.

© 2016 Andrew Bailey

Library and Archives Canada Cataloguing in Publication

Mill, John Stuart, 1806-1873, author
  Utilitarianism / John Stuart Mill ; edited by Andrew Bailey.

"This edition is adapted from The Broadview Anthology of Social
  and Political Thought; General Editors: Andrew Bailey, Samantha
  Brennan, Will Kymlicka, Jacob Levy, Alex Sager, Clark Wolf."
Includes bibliographical references and index.
ISBN 978-1-55481-315-5 (paperback)

  1. Utilitarianism. I. Bailey, Andrew, 1969-, editor II. Title.

B1603.U87 2016   171'.5   C2016-902976-X

Broadview Press handles its own distribution in North America
PO Box 1243, Peterborough, Ontario K9J 7H5, Canada
555 Riverwalk Parkway, Tonawanda, NY 14150, USA
Tel: (705) 743-8990; Fax: (705) 743-8353
email: customerservice@broadviewpress.com

Distribution is handled by Eurospan Group in the UK, Europe, Central Asia, Middle East, Africa, India, Southeast Asia, Central America, South America, and the Caribbean. Distribution is handled by Footprint Books in Australia and New Zealand.

Broadview Press acknowledges the financial support of the Government of Canada through the Canada Book Fund for our publishing activities.

Copy-edited by Martin R. Boyne
Typesetting and assembly: True to Type Inc., Claremont, Canada
Cover Design: Lisa Brawn

PRINTED IN CANADA

Contents

John Stuart Mill, c. 1870.

Introduction

Who Was John Stuart Mill?

John Stuart Mill, the most important British philosopher of the nineteenth century, was born in London in 1806, the eldest son of Scottish utilitarian philosopher and political radical James Mill (1773–1836). His childhood was shaped—some might say, misshaped—by his father's fervent belief in the importance of education. James Mill held that every variation in the talents and capacities of individual human beings could be explained by their education and experiences, and therefore he believed that a proper educational regime, beginning more or less from birth, could train any child to be an almost superhuman intellect. To prove these theories, Mill raised his first son, John Stuart, to be the British radical movement's secret weapon—a prodigious intellect who would be a living demonstration of what could be achieved through properly scientific educational methods, and who would go out into the world to spread the secular gospel of utilitarianism and liberalism.

His father took sole charge of little John Stuart's education from the time when he was a toddler, keeping him isolated from other children (who might be harmful influences) and even from other adults who were not Mill's own philosophical compatriots. John was therefore kept out of schools—which his father believed reinforced ignorant and immoral social attitudes—and educated at home, learning Greek and Latin in the same large study where his father was hard at work on a monumental history of India (and, since no English-Greek dictionary had yet been written, frequently interrupting his father to ask questions about vocabulary). In his autobiography, the younger Mill wrote, "I have no remembrance of the time when I began to learn Greek. I have been told that it was when I was three years old." By the time he was 8—the age at which he began to learn Latin and arithmetic—he had studied much of Greek literature in the original, including all of Herodotus' *Histories* and six dialogues by Plato. At 12 he started on logic and the serious study of philosophy; political economy began at

13; and at 20 he was sent to France for a year to become fluent in that language and to study chemistry and mathematics.[1]

Despite these prodigious achievements, Mill's early life seems not to have been a happy one. He had no toys or children's books—not so much, apparently, because his father forbade them as simply because it never occurred to him to provide them—and John Stuart later remarked that he had never learned to play. Until he was 14 he never really mixed with children his own age at all. An early draft of his autobiography contained the following passage, deleted before publication:

> I believe there is less personal affection in England than in any other country of which I know anything, and I give my father's family not as peculiar in this respect but only as a faithful exemplification of the ordinary fact. That rarity in England, a really warm hearted mother, would in the first place have made the children grow up loving and being loved. But my mother with the very best intentions, only knew how to pass her life in drudging for them ... but to make herself loved, looked up to, or even obeyed, required qualities which she unfortunately did not possess. I thus grew up in the absence of love and in the presence of fear: and many and indelible are the effects of this bringing-up, in the stunting of my moral growth.

At the age of 22, Mill suffered a nervous breakdown and was plunged into suicidal despair. The trigger—according to his autobiography—was a sudden realization that living the life for which his father had trained him could not make him happy:

> ... [I]t occurred to me to put the question directly to myself, "Suppose that all your objects in life were realized; that all the changes in institutions and opinions which you are looking forward to, could be completely effected this very instant: would this be a great joy and happiness to you?" And an irrepressible self-consciousness distinctly answered, "No!" At this my heart sank within me: the whole foundation on which my life was constructed fell down. All my happiness was to have been found in the continual pursuit of this end. The end had ceased to charm,

---

1   At around this time Mill was offered a place at Cambridge University. His father refused it for him, saying he already knew more than Cambridge could ever teach him.

and how could there ever again be any interest in the means? I seemed to have nothing left to live for.

Mill's response to this crisis was not to *abandon* utilitarianism and the radical philosophy of his father, but instead to *modify* the theories by which he had been brought up. He came to adopt the view that "those only are happy ... who have their minds fixed on some object other than their own happiness": that is, true happiness—which, as his father had taught him, is the measure of all action—comes not from the pursuit of one's own happiness in itself, but from living a life filled with concern for the happiness of others and with a love of other things, such as poetry and music, for their own sake. Mill, in fact, claimed his sanity was saved by his discovery of Romantic poetry—especially that of William Wordsworth (1770–1850), Samuel Taylor Coleridge (1772–1834), and Johann Wolfgang von Goethe (1749–1832)—and he later placed great emphasis on the proper development of the emotional and sentimental side of one's character, as well as one's intellect.

In 1830, at 24, Mill began a deeply passionate love affair with a beautiful, vivacious, but married woman, Harriet Hardy Taylor (b. 1807), the wife of John Taylor, a merchant. Mill's relationship with Harriet was central to his life, and she had a great influence on his writings. For 15 years, between 1834 and John Taylor's death in 1849, Harriet and the two Johns lived out a curiously Victorian compromise: Harriet and Mill agreed never to be seen in "society" as a couple—which would cause a scandal—but were allowed by Harriet's husband to go on frequent holidays together. In 1851, two years after her husband's death, Harriet and Mill were finally able to marry, but in 1858, Harriet died of tuberculosis—a disease she probably caught from her new husband, who in turn had probably caught it from his father, who had died of TB in 1836.

Mill never held an academic position, but he spent 35 years working as an administrator for the British East India Company in London. The East India Company, which had also employed Mill's father, was a private trading company formed in 1600 which, by the end of the eighteenth century, had its own army and political service and was effectively administering the sub-continent of India on behalf of the British government. Mill started his career in 1823, at 17, as a clerk in the office of the Examiner of India Correspondence; by 1856 he had become Chief Examiner of India Correspondence, as his father had been before him. In 1858 the East India Company was taken over by the British Crown following the Indian Rebellion of 1857, and Mill retired with a substantial pension.

Mill's work for the company left him plenty of time for his writing, and he was also very active in public life. In 1823 he was arrested for distributing birth-control pamphlets, and in 1825 he helped to found the London Debating Society. In 1824 his father had founded the *Westminster Review*, a quarterly magazine advocating a radically liberal political and social agenda, and John Stuart—only 18 years old at the time of its founding—was a frequent and enthusiastic contributor of articles during its early years. In 1835 he started his own radical periodical, the *London Review*, which soon became the influential *London and Westminster Review* and ran, under his editorship, until 1840. Between 1865 and 1868 Mill was the Liberal Member of Parliament for Westminster, and in 1866 he secured a law guaranteeing freedom of speech in London's Hyde Park.[1] In 1867 he tried, but failed, to amend the second Reform Bill to introduce proportional representation and the vote for women. In 1866—by now something of a "grand old man" of English society—he was made Rector of the University of St. Andrews in Scotland. In 1872 he became godfather to the newborn Bertrand Russell.

Mill died suddenly, from a fever, in 1873, at Aix-en-Provence, France. From about 1860 until 1870 he had been at the peak of his powers and influence. The moral philosopher Henry Sidgwick wrote in 1873, "from about 1860–1865 or thereabouts he ruled England in the region of thought as very few men ever did. I do not expect to see anything like it again." A few decades later the former prime minister James Arthur Balfour noted that the authority of Mill's thought in English universities had been "comparable to that wielded ... by Hegel in Germany and in the middle ages by Aristotle." By the First World War, however, Mill's reputation as a philosopher had suffered a precipitous decline, and he remained in ill-favor in the English-speaking philosophical world until the early 1970s, when new scholarship and changing philosophical fashions made possible a gradual increase in the appreciation of Mill as a major philosophical figure—the finest flowering of nineteenth-century British philosophy, and a precursor for the "naturalist" philosophers of the second half of the twentieth century.

What Was Mill's Overall Philosophical Project?

Mill is important less for the *originality* of his philosophic thought than for his brilliant *synthesis* of several major strands in nineteenth-

---

1   This is the location, since that date, of London's famous Speakers' Corner—a place where "soapbox orators" can say whatever they like with legal impunity.

century (and especially British) thought into a single, compelling, well-developed picture. The main ingredients for his worldview were empiricism, associationism, utilitarianism, and elements of German Romanticism. Together, these elements became what John Skorupski has called Mill's "liberal naturalism."

The bedrock of Mill's philosophy is empiricism: he believed all human knowledge comes ultimately from sense-experience, and his most substantial intellectual project was the attempt to construct a system of empirical knowledge that could underpin not just science but also moral and social affairs. One of his main interests was in showing that empiricism need not lead to skepticism, such as that espoused by Scottish philosopher David Hume (1711–76). Mill's main discussion of the foundation of knowledge and the principles of inference is the massive *System of Logic*, published in six volumes in 1843. In this work he discusses both deductive inference (including mathematics, which Mill argues is—like all human knowledge—reducible to a set of generalizations of relations among sense-experiences) and inductive inference in the natural sciences. He also tries to show how these methods can be applied in politics and the social sciences. Social phenomena, he argues, are just as much the result of causal laws as are natural events, and thus the social sciences—though they will never make us perfectly able to predict human behavior—are capable of putting social policy on an objective footing that goes beyond the mere "intuitions" of conservative common sense.

His prescriptions for scientific practice—today called "Mill's methods"—were highly influential in the development of the philosophy of science in the twentieth century, and his work is still the foundation of modern methodologies for discovering causal laws. The key engine of science, for Mill, is simply *enumerative induction* or generalization from experience. Crudely put, once we have observed a sequence of events that all obey some regularity—ravens that are black, say, or moving magnetic fields being accompanied by an electrical current—we are justified in inferring that all future events of that type will follow the same law.

Mill's work was also a precursor of what is today called "naturalized epistemology." He proposed that all the phenomena of the human mind, including rationality, be treated as the result of the operation of psychological laws acting upon the data of experience. This psychological theory is called *associationism*—since it holds that ideas arise from the psychological associations between sensations—and is particularly defended by Mill in his *Examination of Sir William Hamilton's Philosophy* (1865).

In his own time, Mill was for many years most widely known for his *Principles of Political Economy* (1848), which tried to show that the science of economics—criticized in his day as a "dismal science" that could predict only disaster and starvation—could be reformulated as a progressive force for social progress. Mill pointed out the mismatch between what economics measures and what human beings really value, and this led him to argue for limiting economic growth for the sake of the environment, for controlling populations in order to allow an adequate standard of living for everyone, and for what he considered the economically ideal form of society—a system of worker-owned cooperatives.

Mill's main ethical position, of course, is utilitarianism, which is set out in this edition. As he wrote in his autobiography, of reading Jeremy Bentham's work on utilitarianism (at the age of 15), "it gave unity to my conceptions of things. I now had opinions; a creed, a doctrine, a philosophy; in one among all the best senses of the word, a religion; the inculcation and diffusion of which could be made the principal outward purpose of a life." Mill was also concerned to apply this moral theory to wider questions of social policy. Of all social institutions—including both formal institutions such as laws and churches, and informal ones like social norms—Mill wants to ask: does this institution contribute to human welfare, and does it do so better than any of the alternatives? If the answer is "No," Mill argues, then that institution should (gradually and non-violently) be changed for the better.

Mill's *On Liberty* (1859)—which, during his lifetime, was probably his most notorious writing—is a classic defence of the freedom of thought and discussion, arguing that "the only purpose for which power can be rightfully exercised over any member of a civilized community, against his will, is to prevent harm to others. His own good, either physical or moral, is not a sufficient warrant." This essay was sparked partly by Mill's growing fear of the middle-class conformism (which he saw in America and detected increasing signs of in Britain) that he thought dangerously stifled originality and the critical consideration of ideas. Central to these concerns is Mill's view of human nature as "progressive," as well as the importance of individuality and autonomy. These themes, with their emphasis on the power and importance of the human spirit, were part of what he took from the European Romantic movement.

One of Mill's last works, *The Subjection of Women* (1869), is a classic statement of liberal feminism. Mill argues that women should have just as much freedom as men, and he attacks the conservative view that women and men have different "natures" that suit them for different spheres of life by arguing that no one could possibly know this—since all knowledge comes only from experience—unless women were first allowed to throw off their oppression and, over several generations, try to do all the things that men were allowed to do.

What Is the Structure of This Reading?

Utilitarianism was not written as a scholarly treatise but as a sequence of articles, published in a monthly magazine and intended for the general educated reader: consequently, although *Utilitarianism* is philosophically weighty and—just below the surface—often difficult, its overall structure is quite straightforward. Mill begins by making some general remarks in the first chapter, attacking moral intuitionism and suggesting, among other things, that the principle of utilitarianism has always had a major tacit influence on moral beliefs. In Chapter 2 he defines utilitarianism, attempts to head off several common misunderstandings of the doctrine, and raises and responds to about ten possible objections to the theory (such as that utilitarianism is a godless morality worthy only of pigs, or alternatively that it sets an impracticably high standard that can never be attained by mere mortal human beings). In the third chapter, Mill considers the question of moral motivation and discusses how people might come to feel themselves morally bound by the principles of utilitarianism, arguing that utilitarianism is grounded in the natural social feelings of humanity. In Chapter 4 Mill sets out to give a positive "proof" (insofar as that is possible) for the claim that utilitarianism is the correct moral theory: he argues, first, that one's own happiness is desirable to oneself; second that it follows that happiness is simply desirable in itself, no matter whose it is; and third that *only* happiness is intrinsically desirable. It is this third stage in the argument that takes up most of the chapter. The final chapter of *Utilitarianism* is a long discussion dealing with the relationship between utilitarianism and justice.

Some Useful Background Information

1. Mill frames much of *Utilitarianism* in terms of a debate between two basic positions on the nature of morality: the "intuitive" school and the "inductive" school. The intuitionists, whom Mill attacks, believed that ethical facts—though as real and as objectively true as any others—are *non-empirical*: that is, moral truths cannot be detected or confirmed using the five senses, but instead are known through the

special faculty of "moral intuition." This philosophical position was represented in Mill's time by, among others, Sir William Hamilton (1788–1856) and William Whewell (1794–1866), and Mill's frequent criticism of the notion of "transcendental" moral facts is directed at intuitionists such as them. Mill considered intuitionism to be not only false but also a serious obstacle to social and moral progress. He thought the claim that (educated) human beings can "just tell" which moral principles are true, without needing or being able to cite evidence for these beliefs, tended to act as a disguise for prejudice and social conservatism. Mill's own moral methodology, by contrast, was what he called "inductive": he believed that *all* human knowledge, including ethical knowledge, comes ultimately from sense experience and therefore that moral judgments must be explained and defended by showing their connections to actual human experience.

2. The notion of *happiness* is a very important part of Mill's moral philosophy, so it is useful to be clear about exactly what his theory of happiness is. Because of Mill's empiricist and associationist philosophical upbringing, it was most natural for him to adopt a kind of hedonistic view of happiness. In keeping with his emphasis on sense experience as the key to understanding knowledge and the mind, Mill thinks of happiness as a kind of *pleasurable mental state* (*hēdonē* is the classical Greek word for "pleasure"). For Mill, a happy life is, roughly, one filled with as many pleasurable sensations, and as few painful ones, as possible.

Mill followed his philosophical predecessors in thinking that pleasurable experiences can be classified according to their duration and their intensity: thus rational people seeking their own happiness will aim to arrange their lives so that, over time, they will have more longer-lasting pleasures than short-lived ones, and more intense pleasures than dilute ones. For example, the initial painfulness of learning the violin might be more than offset by the intense and long-lasting pleasure of playing it well.[1] In addition, however, Mill distinguishes between different *qualities* of pleasure. For Mill

---

1 Mill's mentor Jeremy Bentham (1748–1832) even proposed what he called a "felicific calculus": a mathematical system for measuring the total net quantity of pleasure to be expected from a given course of action. Roughly, calculate the balance of pleasure and pain that would accompany a particular outcome of your actions—taking into account their intensity and duration—and then multiply this number by the probability of that outcome actually occurring. This yields what Bentham called the "expected utility" of an action. The rational agent—according to Bentham—acts in a way that has the greatest expected utility. See Chapter 4 of Bentham's *An Introduction to the Principles of Morals and Legislation* in the Appendix.

(unlike, say, Bentham), pleasure is not just one type of mental sensation but comes in "higher" and "lower" varieties. For example, according to Mill, the pleasant feeling that accompanies advanced intellectual or creative activity is a more valuable kind of pleasure—even if it is no more intense or long-lasting—than that which comes from physical satisfactions like eating and sex.

3. One of Mill's philosophical presuppositions that is significant for his moral and social philosophy is *individualism*. Mill assumed that individual persons are the basic unit of political analysis—that social structures are nothing more than constructions out of these individuals and are nothing over and above particular people and the relations between them. It follows that the analysis of social phenomena must be approached through a study of the actions and intentions of individuals, and similarly that social change is possible only through a large number of changes to individual people. What matters to Mill is not "the general happiness" in some abstract sense, but the happiness of large numbers of individual human beings. He views social institutions as merely *instruments* for benefiting all these people. Furthermore, for Mill (influenced, as he was, by European Romanticism), there is a special kind of *value* in individuality: the particular uniqueness of each person is a thing to be treasured in itself.

Some Common Misconceptions

1. For Mill, mere *exemption* from pain is not itself a good. He holds that pleasure is the only good, and pain the only bad, and the overall goodness of states of affairs consists in the *balance* of pleasure over pain. The absence of pain is thus merely morally neutral, unless it is accompanied by the positive presence of pleasure.

2. Mill is not arguing that people already *do* act in order to produce the greatest happiness of the greatest number: he is arguing that we *should*. He is not merely describing an already prevalent moral psychology, but arguing for a certain set of moral attitudes that he thinks we ought to cultivate in ourselves and in society in general.

3. Utilitarianism is a theory of actions and not motives. It does not require that people *intend* to maximize utility but rather that their behavior, in fact, does so. Mill insists that the criterion for what makes an action right is that it maximize utility; it does not follow from this that all our actions must have the conscious goal of maximiz-

ing utility. In fact, there is a good case to be made that a community where everyone is *trying* to maximize utility all the time would actually be self-defeating and a much less happy society than it would be if people acted from other motivations. If this is right, it would follow that, according to utilitarianism itself, it would be immoral to be always consciously trying to maximize utility. This is not a paradox or a problem for the theory, however; it simply shows there is a difference between the criterion of right action and the best advice one can give moral agents for actually meeting that criterion.

Actions, according to Mill, include within themselves two parts: an *intention* (which is different from a motive—it is not *why* the action is done but *what* the action is intended to achieve), and the action's *effects*. Mill sometimes appeals to differences of intention to distinguish between kinds of actions (as in his Chapter 3 footnote about a tyrant rescuing a drowning man), but, strictly speaking, only the *effects* or consequences of an action can be morally relevant in Mill's view.

4. One common complaint against utilitarianism is that it makes *every* action, no matter how trivial, a moral issue: pretty much everything we do (e.g., getting a haircut) will have *some* effect on someone's pleasure and pain, and so it appears we have a moral duty to ensure we *always* act in such a way as to maximize the general happiness—and this, to say the least, would seem to put a bit of a strain on everyday life. However, even if this is, in fact, an implication of Mill's utilitarian theory, he did not intend to commit us to such an onerous regime. Something that Mill writes elsewhere (in *Auguste Comte and Positivism* [1865]) is illuminating in this regard: "It is not good that persons should be bound, by other people's opinion, to do everything that they would deserve praise for doing. There is a standard of altruism to which all should be required to come up, and a degree beyond which it is not obligatory, but meritorious."

5. Despite how *Utilitarianism* can strike us today, in the aftermath of the grand and often massively destructive social-engineering projects of the twentieth century, Mill was actually a bitter foe of what might be called "social constructivism." He emphatically did *not* see society as merely a machine built to help human beings to live together, a machine that can be broken into bits and reconstructed if it is not working optimally, and one where the rational, technical vision of collective planners should override individual initiative

in the public good. On the contrary, Mill was very much an individualist and a humanist. He saw society as built from the actions of separate individual human beings and held that it is a kind of historical "consensus" that has created traditions and cultural practices that are continually but gradually evolving over time. Mill's vision for the reform of society, then, was not the imposition of central planning, but instead the gradual construction of a set of cultural norms—including, especially, a progressive educational system—to create human beings with the best possible moral character.

How Important and Influential Is This Work?

John Stuart Mill did not *invent* utilitarianism (and never pretended to have done so). Indeed, he was brought up by people who already considered themselves utilitarians. Mill's importance to utilitarianism is that he gave it what is arguably its single greatest and most influential formulation, in the essay *Utilitarianism*. It is this work that, ever since it was written, has been the starting point for both defenders and foes of utilitarianism. Furthermore, utilitarianism is itself a very important and influential moral theory. Along with Marxism, it was arguably the most prevalent moral theory among philosophers, economists, political scientists, and other social theorists for much of the twentieth century (completely eclipsing—or in some cases, as with G.E. Moore's moral philosophy, absorbing—the moral "intuitionism" that Mill saw as his theory's main competitor in 1861). Utilitarianism's influence has waned since the 1970s and it has been subjected to several damaging philosophical attacks, but it is still, uncontroversially, one of the four or five most discussed and appealed-to moral theories in contemporary philosophical discourse.

Suggestions for Critical Reflection

1. One of the attractions of utilitarianism, it is often supposed, is that it is "scientific" or objective in a way that intuitionism (or other ethical theories such as Kantianism, or virtue theory) is not. The Greatest Happiness Principle apparently provides a quasi-mathematical, bias-free, and theoretically motivated way of working out what we ought to do in literally any moral situation. But is this really so? For example, can the pleasures and pains of sentient creatures really be "objectively" measured and compared, in order to calculate the net effect of actions on utility? Even if pleasures

and pains are measurable, do you think all the consequences of an action can be properly predicted and measured? How serious are these problems for utilitarianism?

2. Does Mill's notion of "higher" or more "noble" pleasure make sense? How could the "nobility" of an experience add to the pleasure of it? Why couldn't an experience be noble but not pleasant? In that case, would Mill have to say that it is still valuable? In other words, is Mill *really* a hedonist (i.e., someone who thinks that only pleasure has intrinsic value—and only pain intrinsic disvalue)?

3. An influential criticism of the hedonistic component of utilitarianism was invented by philosopher Robert Nozick (1938–2002) and is called the "experience machine." The experience machine is a fictional device that keeps your body alive in a tank of fluids, for a normal human life-span, all the while stimulating your brain so that you continuously feel as if you are having the most pleasant and satisfying experiences imaginable. Since—properly designed—this would be an utterly reliable way of maximizing the quality and number of pleasant sensations during your lifetime, it seems that the utilitarian is forced to conclude that it would be our *moral duty* to plug ourselves into one of these machines (especially if they are such reliable and long-lasting devices that nearly everyone can be plugged in at the same time). But Nozick argues that this result is clearly unsatisfactory: surely there is more to a valuable life than a mere succession of pleasant experiences, and so utilitarianism must be a faulty moral theory. What do you think about Nozick's argument? What exactly does it suggest is wrong with utilitarianism (or at least Mill's version of the theory)? Could this problem—if it is a problem—be fixed?

4. Roger Crisp has called the third paragraph of the fourth chapter of *Utilitarianism* "the most notorious [passage] in Mill's writings" (p. 73 of the *Routledge Philosophy Guidebook to Mill on Utilitarianism*). In it Mill compares desirability with visibility in an effort to argue that desire is a faculty that reveals what we morally ought to do. The most famous and apparently devastating criticism of this argument came from G.E. Moore in 1903: "The fact is that 'desirable' does not mean 'able to be desired' as 'visible' means 'able to be seen.' The desirable means simply what *ought* to be desired or deserves to be desired." How does Moore's complaint cause problems for Mill's argument? Does Mill really make the mistake

Moore is suggesting? If Mill's own arguments fail to show that we *ought* to desire happiness, is there any other way a utilitarian could consistently argue for this claim? Does utilitarianism need to provide arguments for it?

5. How well does Mill refute moral egoism? That is, does his argument show that I ought to care about *everyone*'s happiness, and not just my own? Does he have an *argument* for the "impartiality" component of utilitarianism? Does he need one?

6. Is Mill right that we desire *only* happiness? In other words, is his claim that, "to desire anything, except in proportion as the idea of it is pleasant, is a physical and metaphysical impossibility," a plausible one? If he is wrong, how seriously does this undercut his argument for the truth of utilitarianism? For example, what about Mill's own example of virtue: is he right in arguing that we value our own virtue only as a "part" of our happiness?

7. Utilitarianism is a kind of moral theory that is sometimes called "welfarist": for such theories, the only thing of intrinsic value is the welfare of moral agents (according to Mill, sentient beings). One consequence of welfarism is that *nothing else* is of intrinsic value. Thus, for example, the beauty of art and nature, ecological sustainability, scientific knowledge, justice, equality, loyalty, kindness, or self-sacrifice—none of these things have any value in themselves but are valuable *only* insofar as they increase the welfare of sentient creatures (and are actually *immoral* if they reduce this welfare). Does this seem to be an acceptable consequence of a moral theory?

8. Utilitarianism is often accused of being an extremely demanding moral theory. According to utilitarianism, a certain unit of pleasure or pain should matter *equally* to me whether it belongs to me, to a member of my family, to a stranger halfway across the world, or even to an animal. Utilitarianism requires us to maximize overall happiness, and does not allow us to think of the happiness of ourselves and our friends as being especially important. If you or I were to spend all of our free time, and use almost all of our money, working to help victims of famine and other natural disasters around the world, this might well produce more overall utility than the lives we currently lead. If so, then utilitarianism apparently commits us to a moral *duty* to behave in this way, and we are being

flat-out *immoral* in spending time with our families or watching movies. Is this acceptable? If not, what is wrong with it?

9. According to utilitarianism, should we be morally responsible for all the consequences of our actions, including the unforeseen ones? What would Mill say? Are we just as responsible for *not* doing things that could have prevented great pain? For example, according to utilitarianism, am I equally morally deficient if I fail to give money to charity as I am if I send poisoned food to famine-stricken areas (supposing the outcomes in terms of human death and suffering would be the same)?

10. Act (or "direct") utilitarianism is the view that one should act in any circumstance so as to produce the greatest overall balance of pleasure over pain. (You would have a moral duty to break an important promise to your best friend if it would increase overall utility by even a tiny amount, for example.) Rule (or "indirect") utilitarianism, on the other hand, is the view that one should act in accordance with certain moral rules, rules fixed as those which, over time, can be expected to maximize utility if they are generally followed. (For example, you should never break an important promise, even if you can foresee that keeping it, in a particular case, will cause far more pain than pleasure.) Is Mill an act or rule utilitarian? Which is the better theory? Is *either* version attractive and, if not, can you think of a third option for utilitarianism?

11. According to utilitarianism, *how* should we maximize utility? Should we aim to maximize the *total* utility of the world, the *average* utility, or what? (For example, if we chose to maximize total utility, we might be morally obliged to aim for an extremely large population, even if each member has only a low level of happiness; on the other hand, if we opt for the highest possible average utility we might be committed to keeping the population small and select, perhaps killing, before birth, people who look as though they might drag the average down.) What would Mill say?

12. Mill thought utilitarianism to be the one true fundamental moral theory and to be consistent with (what is right in) the moral theories of Aristotle and Kant. If you are familiar with Aristotle's and Kant's ethical views, consider whether utilitarianism is in fact consistent with them. For example, could Kant accept that consequences are what is morally important about our actions?

Suggestions for Further Reading

Mill's writings have been published as *The Collected Works of John Stuart Mill*, under the general editorship of John Robson (33 volumes, University of Toronto Press, 1963–91). Mill's *Autobiography* is available from Penguin (1990), and a good edition of his *On Liberty*, with interesting supplemental material, was edited by Leonard Kahn and published by Broadview Press (2014). Jeremy Bentham's *An Introduction to the Principles of Morals and Legislation*, edited by J.H. Burns and H.L.A. Hart (Oxford University Press, 1996) is also essential reading for any serious student of Mill's *Utilitarianism* (note that chapters 1 and 4 of that work are included as an appendix in this edition).

Three worthwhile books about Mill's philosophy as a whole are Alan Ryan's *J.S. Mill* (Routledge & Kegan Paul, 1974) and *The Philosophy of John Stuart Mill* (Prometheus Books, 1990), and John Skorupski's *John Stuart Mill* (Routledge, 1989). Roger Crisp has written a *Routledge Philosophy Guidebook to Mill on Utilitarianism* (Routledge, 1997); there is a *Blackwell Guide to Mill's Utilitarianism* (Blackwell, 2006), edited by Henry R. West; and there are a number of good books on Mill's moral theory, including Fred Berger, *Happiness, Justice, and Freedom: The Moral and Political Philosophy of John Stuart Mill* (University of California Press, 1984); David O. Brink, *Mill's Progressive Principles* (Oxford University Press, 2013); Wendy Donner, *The Liberal Self: John Stuart Mill's Moral and Political Philosophy* (Cornell University Press, 1992); David Lyons, *Rights, Welfare, and Mill's Moral Theory* (Oxford University Press, 1994); and Bernard Semmel, *John Stuart Mill and the Pursuit of Virtue* (Yale University Press, 1984).

G.E. Moore's attack on Mill's argument for utilitarianism appears in *Principia Ethica*, edited by Thomas Baldwin (Cambridge University Press, 1994, originally published 1903). An early defence of Mill against this attack is James Seth's "The Alleged Fallacies in Mill's 'Utilitarianism,'" *Philosophical Review* 17 (1908); more recently, Necip Fikri Alican has written a book called *Mill's Principle of Utility: A Defense of John Stuart Mill's Notorious Proof* (Rodopi, 1994). Robert Nozick's "experience machine" argument was published in *Anarchy, State, and Utopia* (Basic Books, 1974, pp. 42–45).

Three useful collections of essays about Mill are J.B. Schneewind (ed.), *Mill: A Collection of Critical Essays* (Doubleday, 1968); David Lyons (ed.), *Mill's 'Utilitarianism': Critical Essays* (Rowman and Littlefield, 1997); and John Skorupski (ed.), *The Cambridge Companion to Mill* (Cambridge University Press, 1998). Other useful articles include J.O. Urmson, "The Interpretation of the Moral Philosophy of

J.S. Mill," *Philosophical Quarterly* 3 (1953); Rex Martin, "A Defence of *Mill's Qualitative Hedonism*," *Philosophy* 47 (1972); R.M. Adams, "Motive Utilitarianism," *Journal of Philosophy* 73 (1976); Henry R. West, "Mill's Qualitative Hedonism," *Philosophy* 51 (1976); Roger Crisp, "Utilitarianism and the Life of Virtue," *Philosophical Quarterly* 42 (1992); and L.W. Sumner, "Welfare, Happiness and Pleasure," *Utilitas* 4 (1992).

Finally, there is a substantial literature on the moral theory of utilitarianism in its own right. Perhaps the best starting point is J.J.C. Smart and Bernard Williams, *Utilitarianism: For and Against* (Cambridge University Press, 1973). James Griffin's "Modern Utilitarianism," *Revue Internationale de Philosophie* 141 (1982), is a very useful review of the modern development of the theory. The following books are also valuable: Richard Brandt, *Morality, Utilitarianism, and Rights* (Cambridge University Press, 1992); David Lyons, *Forms and Limits of Utilitarianism* (Oxford University Press, 1965); Derek Parfit, *Reasons and Persons* (Oxford University Press, 1986); Anthony Quinton, *Utilitarian Ethics* (Open Court, 1989); Geoffrey Scarre, *Utilitarianism* (Routledge, 1996); Samuel Scheffler (ed.), *Consequentialism and Its Critics* (Oxford University Press, 1988); Samuel Scheffler, *The Rejection of Consequentialism* (Oxford University Press, 1994); Amartya Sen and Bernard Williams (eds.), *Utilitarianism and Beyond* (Cambridge University Press, 1982); William Shaw, *Contemporary Ethics: Taking Account of Utilitarianism* (Blackwell, 1999); Julia Driver, *Consequentialism* (Routledge, 2011); and Ben Eggleston and Dale Miller (eds.), *The Cambridge Companion to Utilitarianism* (Cambridge University Press, 2014).

Utilitarianism

Utilitarianism[1]

Chapter 1: General Remarks

There are few circumstances among those which make up the present
condition of human knowledge, more unlike what might have been
expected, or more significant of the backward state in which speculation on the most important subjects still lingers, than the little progress
which has been made in the decision of the controversy respecting the
criterion of right and wrong. From the dawn of philosophy, the question concerning the *summum bonum*,[2] or, what is the same thing, concerning the foundation of morality, has been accounted the main
problem in speculative thought, has occupied the most gifted intel-
lects, and divided them into sects and schools, carrying on a vigorous
warfare against one another. And after more than two thousand years
the same discussions continue, philosophers are still ranged under the
same contending banners, and neither thinkers nor mankind at large
seem nearer to being unanimous on the subject, than when the youth
Socrates[3] listened to the old Protagoras,[4] and asserted (if Plato's dia-

1   *Utilitarianism* was first published in 1861 as a series of three essays in volume 64
    of *Fraser's Magazine*. It was first published as a book in 1863; this text is from
    the fourth edition, published in 1871 (by Longmans, Green, Reader, and Dyer),
    the last to be printed in Mill's lifetime.
2   Latin: "The highest good": that thing which is an end-in-itself, which gives every-
    thing else its value, and the achievement of which is (arguably) the goal of an eth-
    ical system. Candidates for the "highest good" might be—indeed, historically
    have been—pleasure, human flourishing, the rational comprehension of reality, or
    God.
3   Socrates (469–399 BCE) was a highly influential philosopher from Athens who—
    particularly through his great impact on Plato—is often thought to be the main
    originator of the western philosophical tradition. He wrote nothing himself but ap-
    pears as a character in nearly all of Plato's dialogues.
4   Protagoras (c. 490–c. 420 BCE) was the greatest of the Sophist philosophers—
    itinerant teachers of rhetoric and practical philosophy—and is most famous for his
    doctrine that "Man is the measure of all things," which is usually interpreted as an
    extreme form of relativism.

logue be grounded on a real conversation[1]) the theory of utilitarianism against the popular morality of the so-called sophist.

It is true that similar confusion and uncertainty, and in some cases similar discordance, exist respecting the first principles of all the sciences, not excepting that which is deemed the most certain of them, mathematics; without much impairing, generally indeed without impairing at all, the trustworthiness of the conclusions of those sciences. An apparent anomaly, the explanation of which is, that the detailed doctrines of a science are not usually deduced from, nor depend for their evidence upon, what are called its first principles. Were it not so, there would be no science more precarious, or whose conclusions were more insufficiently made out, than algebra; which derives none of its certainty from what are commonly taught to learners as its elements, since these, as laid down by some of its most eminent teachers, are as full of fictions as English law, and of mysteries as theology. The truths which are ultimately accepted as the first principles of a science, are really the last results of metaphysical analysis, practised on the elementary notions with which the science is conversant; and their relation to the science is not that of foundations to an edifice, but of roots to a tree, which may perform their office equally well though they be never dug down to and exposed to light. But though in science the particular truths precede the general theory, the contrary might be expected to be the case with a practical art, such as morals or legislation. All action is for the sake of some end, and rules of action, it seems natural to suppose, must take their whole character and colour from the end to which they are subservient. When we engage in a pursuit, a clear and precise conception of what we are pursuing would seem to be the first thing we need, instead of the last we are to look forward to. A test of right and wrong must be the means, one would think, of ascertaining what is right or wrong, and not a consequence of having already ascertained it.

The difficulty is not avoided by having recourse to the popular theory of a natural faculty, a sense or instinct, informing us of right and wrong. For—besides that the existence of such a moral instinct is itself one of the matters in dispute—those believers in it who have any

---

1 Mill first read this dialogue—called the *Protagoras*—during the "more advanced" period of his education (after he had reached the age of 12). It is questionable whether Socrates does indeed put forward utilitarianism in that dialogue (and almost certain that he was not himself a utilitarian). Mill, however, was always anxious to portray utilitarianism as a doctrine already widespread in the history of philosophy (and especially in ancient Greek philosophy: in *On Liberty*, for example, he describes Aristotle's ethics as "judicious utilitarianism").

pretensions to philosophy, have been obliged to abandon the idea that it discerns what is right or wrong in the particular case in hand, as our other senses discern the sight or sound actually present. Our moral faculty, according to all those of its interpreters who are entitled to the name of thinkers, supplies us only with the general principles of moral judgments; it is a branch of our reason, not of our sensitive faculty;[1] and must be looked to for the abstract doctrines of morality, not for perception of it in the concrete. The intuitive, no less than what may be termed the inductive, school of ethics, insists on the necessity of general laws. They both agree that the morality of an individual action is not a question of direct perception, but of the application of a law to an individual case. They recognise also, to a great extent, the same moral laws; but differ as to their evidence, and the source from which they derive their authority. According to the one opinion, the principles of morals are evident *a priori*,[2] requiring nothing to command assent, except that the meaning of the terms be understood. According to the other doctrine, right and wrong, as well as truth and falsehood, are questions of observation and experience. But both hold equally that morality must be deduced from principles; and the intuitive school affirm as strongly as the inductive, that there is a science of morals. Yet they seldom attempt to make out a list of the *a priori* principles which are to serve as the premises of the science; still more rarely do they make any effort to reduce those various principles to one first principle, or common ground of obligation. They either assume the ordinary precepts[3] of morals as of *a priori* authority, or they lay down as the common groundwork of those maxims, some generality much less obviously authoritative than the maxims themselves, and which has never succeeded in gaining popular acceptance. Yet to support their pretensions there ought either to be some one fundamental principle or law, at the root of all morality, or if there be several, there should be a determinate order of precedence among them; and the one principle, or the rule for deciding between the various principles when they conflict, ought to be self-evident.

To inquire how far the bad effects of this deficiency have been mitigated in practice, or to what extent the moral beliefs of mankind have been vitiated or made uncertain by the absence of any distinct recognition of an ultimate standard, would imply a complete survey and

---

1   Mill means our faculty of sensation.

2   That which is evident *a priori* is obviously true, independent of any actual experience. ("*A priori*" means knowable prior to experience.)

3   A precept is an instruction or command prescribing a particular course of action (such as "always tell the truth" or "do not commit adultery").

criticism, of past and present ethical doctrine. It would, however, be easy to show that whatever steadiness or consistency these moral beliefs have attained, has been mainly due to the tacit influence of a standard not recognised. Although the non-existence of an acknowledged first principle has made ethics not so much a guide as a consecration of men's actual sentiments, still, as men's sentiments, both of favour and of aversion, are greatly influenced by what they suppose to be the effects of things upon their happiness, the principle of utility, or as Bentham[1] latterly called it, the greatest happiness principle, has had a large share in forming the moral doctrines even of those who most scornfully reject its authority. Nor is there any school of thought which refuses to admit that the influence of actions on happiness is a most material and even predominant consideration in many of the details of morals, however unwilling to acknowledge it as the fundamental principle of morality, and the source of moral obligation. I might go much further, and say that to all those *a priori* moralists who deem it necessary to argue at all, utilitarian arguments are indispensable. It is not my present purpose to criticise these thinkers; but I cannot help referring, for illustration, to a systematic treatise by one of the most illustrious of them, the *Metaphysics of Ethics*, by Kant.[2] This remarkable man, whose system of thought will long remain one of the landmarks in the history of philosophical speculation, does, in the treatise in question, lay down a universal first principle as the origin and ground of moral obligation; it is this: "So act, that the rule on which thou actest would admit of being adopted as a law by all rational beings." But when he begins to deduce from this precept any of the actual duties of morality, he fails, almost grotesquely, to show that there would be any contradiction, any logical (not to say physical) impossibility, in the adoption by all rational beings of the most outrageously immoral rules of conduct. All he shows is that the *consequences* of their universal adoption would be such as no one would choose to incur.

---

1   Jeremy Bentham (1748–1832) was an English philosopher of law and ethics who is usually thought of as the founder of utilitarianism, which he intended as a coherent and sensible foundation for the large-scale reform of social and legal policy. His main theoretical work was *An Introduction to the Principles of Morals and Legislation*, published in 1789 (chapters 1 and 4 of which are included in this edition), and it is in this book that the Greatest Happiness Principle was first clearly formulated and defended. It was while reading a French edition of Bentham's *Principles of Morals* in 1821 that, according to Mill's autobiography, he was permanently "converted" to utilitarianism.

2   Mill is actually thinking of *Foundations of the Metaphysics of Morals*, by the German philosopher Immanuel Kant (1724–1804).

On the present occasion, I shall, without further discussion of the other theories, attempt to contribute something towards the understanding and appreciation of the Utilitarian or Happiness theory, and towards such proof as it is susceptible of. It is evident that this cannot be proof in the ordinary and popular meaning of the term. Questions of ultimate ends are not amenable to direct proof. Whatever can be proved to be good, must be so by being shown to be a means to something admitted to be good without proof. The medical art is proved to be good by its conducing to health; but how is it possible to prove that health is good? The art of music is good, for the reason, among others, that it produces pleasure; but what proof is it possible to give that pleasure is good? If, then, it is asserted that there is a comprehensive formula, including all things which are in themselves good, and that whatever else is good, is not so as an end, but as a mean, the formula may be accepted or rejected, but is not a subject of what is commonly understood by proof. We are not, however, to infer that its acceptance or rejection must depend on blind impulse, or arbitrary choice. There is a larger meaning of the word proof, in which this question is as amenable to it as any other of the disputed questions of philosophy. The subject is within the cognisance[1] of the rational faculty; and neither does that faculty deal with it solely in the way of intuition. Considerations may be presented capable of determining the intellect either to give or withhold its assent to the doctrine; and this is equivalent to proof.

We shall examine presently of what nature are these considerations; in what manner they apply to the case, and what rational grounds, therefore, can be given for accepting or rejecting the utilitarian formula. But it is a preliminary condition of rational acceptance or rejection, that the formula should be correctly understood. I believe that the very imperfect notion ordinarily formed of its meaning, is the chief obstacle which impedes its reception; and that could it be cleared, even from only the grosser misconceptions, the question would be greatly simplified, and a large proportion of its difficulties removed. Before, therefore, I attempt to enter into the philosophical grounds which can be given for assenting to the utilitarian standard, I shall offer some illustrations of the doctrine itself; with the view of showing more clearly what it is, distinguishing it from what it is not, and disposing of such of the practical objections to it as either originate in, or are closely connected with, mistaken interpretations of its meaning. Having thus prepared the ground, I shall afterwards endeavour to throw such light as I can upon the question, considered as one of philosophical theory.

---

1   Sphere of concern or awareness.

Chapter 2: What Utilitarianism Is

A passing remark is all that needs be given to the ignorant blunder of supposing that those who stand up for utility as the test of right and wrong, use the term in that restricted and merely colloquial sense in which utility is opposed to pleasure. An apology is due to the philosophical opponents of utilitarianism, for even the momentary appearance of confounding them with any one capable of so absurd a misconception; which is the more extraordinary, inasmuch as the contrary accusation, of referring everything to pleasure, and that too in its grossest form, is another of the common charges against utilitarianism: and, as has been pointedly remarked by an able writer,[1] the same sort of persons, and often the very same persons, denounce the theory "as impracticably dry when the word utility precedes the word pleasure, and as too practicably voluptuous when the word pleasure precedes the word utility." Those who know anything about the matter are aware that every writer, from Epicurus[2] to Bentham, who maintained the theory of utility, meant by it, not something to be contradistinguished from pleasure, but pleasure itself, together with exemption from pain; and instead of opposing the useful to the agreeable or the ornamental, have always declared that the useful means these, among other things. Yet the common herd, including the herd of writers, not only in newspapers and periodicals, but in books of weight and pretension, are perpetually falling into this shallow mistake. Having caught up the word utilitarian, while knowing nothing whatever about it but its sound, they habitually express by it the rejection, or the neglect, of pleasure in some of its forms; of beauty, of ornament, or of amusement. Nor is the term thus ignorantly misapplied solely in disparagement, but occasionally in compliment; as though it implied superiority to frivolity and the mere pleasures of the moment. And this perverted use is the only one in which the word is popularly known, and the one from which the new generation are acquiring their sole notion of its meaning. Those who introduced the word, but who had for

---

1   The identity of this writer remains mysterious.

2   Epicurus (341–270 BCE) was a Greek philosopher and founder of the loosely-knit school of thought called Epicureanism. A central plank of this doctrine is—as the modern connotations of the word "epicurean" suggest—that the good life is one filled with pleasure. Indeed, for Epicurus, the only rational goal in life is one's own pleasure. However, contrary to the popular association of "Epicureanism" with mere sensual self-indulgence, Epicurus placed much greater emphasis on stable, non-sensory pleasures (say, the pleasures of friendship and psychological contentment) and also stressed the importance of dispensing with unnecessary desires, harmful fears (such as the fear of death), and hollow gratifications.

many years discontinued it as a distinctive appellation, may well feel themselves called upon to resume it, if by doing so they can hope to contribute anything towards rescuing it from this utter degradation.[1]

The creed which accepts as the foundation of morals, Utility, or the Greatest Happiness Principle, holds that actions are right in propor- tion as they tend to promote happiness, wrong as they tend to produce the reverse of happiness. By happiness is intended pleasure, and the absence of pain; by unhappiness, pain, and the privation of pleasure. To give a clear view of the moral standard set up by the theory, much more requires to be said; in particular, what things it includes in the ideas of pain and pleasure; and to what extent this is left an open question. But these supplementary explanations do not affect the theory of life on which this theory of morality is grounded—namely, that pleasure, and freedom from pain, are the only things desirable as ends; and that all desirable things (which are as numerous in the utilitarian as in any other scheme) are desirable either for the pleasure inherent in themselves, or as means to the promotion of pleasure and the prevention of pain.

Now, such a theory of life excites in many minds, and among them in some of the most estimable in feeling and purpose, inveterate dislike. To suppose that life has (as they express it) no higher end than pleasure—no better and nobler object of desire and pursuit—they designate as utterly mean and grovelling; as a doctrine worthy only of swine, to whom the followers of Epicurus were, at a very early period, contemptuously likened;[2] and modern holders of the doctrine are occasionally made the subject of equally polite comparisons by its German, French, and English assailants.

When thus attacked, the Epicureans have always answered, that it is not they, but their accusers, who represent human nature in a degrading light; since the accusation supposes human beings to be capable of no pleasures except those of which swine are capable. If this

---

1   [Mill's note:] The author of this essay has reason for believing himself to be the first person who brought the word utilitarian into use. He did not invent it, but adopted it from a passing expression in Mr. Galt's *Annals of the Parish*. After using it as a designation for several years, he and others abandoned it from a growing dislike to anything resembling a badge or watchword of sectarian distinction. But as a name for one single opinion, not a set of opinions—to denote the recognition of utility as a standard, not any particular way of applying it—the term supplies a want in the language, and offers, in many cases, a convenient mode of avoiding tiresome circumlocution. [John Galt (1779–1839) was a Scottish novelist and entrepreneur. *Annals of the Parish* was published in 1821.]

2   For example, in Diogenes Laertius's *Lives of Eminent Philosophers*, written c. 230 CE.

supposition were true, the charge could not be gainsaid,[1] but would then be no longer an imputation; for if the sources of pleasure were precisely the same to human beings and to swine, the rule of life which is good enough for the one would be good enough for the other. The comparison of the Epicurean life to that of beasts is felt as degrading, precisely because a beast's pleasures do not satisfy a human being's conceptions of happiness. Human beings have faculties more elevated than the animal appetites, and when once made conscious of them, do not regard anything as happiness which does not include their gratification. I do not, indeed, consider the Epicureans to have been by any means faultless in drawing out their scheme of consequences from the utilitarian principle. To do this in any sufficient manner, many Stoic,[2] as well as Christian elements require to be included. But there is no known Epicurean theory of life which does not assign to the pleasures of the intellect, of the feelings and imagination, and of the moral sentiments, a much higher value as pleasures than to those of mere sensation. It must be admitted, however, that utilitarian writers in general have placed the superiority of mental over bodily pleasures chiefly in the greater permanency, safety, uncostliness, etc., of the former—that is, in their circumstantial advantages rather than in their intrinsic nature. And on all these points utilitarians have fully proved their case; but they might have taken the other, and, as it may be called, higher ground, with entire consistency. It is quite compatible with the principle of utility to recognise the fact, that some *kinds* of pleasure are more desirable and more valuable than others. It would be absurd that while, in estimating all other things, quality is considered as well as quantity, the estimation of pleasures should be supposed to depend on quantity alone.

If I am asked, what I mean by difference of quality in pleasures, or what makes one pleasure more valuable than another, merely as a pleasure, except its being greater in amount, there is but one possible answer. Of two pleasures, if there be one to which all or almost all who have experience of both give a decided preference, irrespective of any feeling of moral obligation to prefer it, that is the more desirable pleasure. If one of the two is, by those who are competently acquainted

---

1   Denied.

2   Stoicism was, with Epicureanism, one of the two main strands of "Hellenistic" philosophy (roughly, that associated with Greek culture during the 300 years after the death of Alexander the Great in 323 BCE). Its main ethical doctrine was that the wise and virtuous person accepts, with calm indifference, their place in the impartial, rational, inevitable order of the universe—even if it is their fate to suffer hardship or painful death—but also works dutifully to foster a social order that mirrors the rational order of the cosmos.

with both, placed so far above the other that they prefer it, even though knowing it to be attended with a greater amount of discontent, and would not resign it for any quantity of the other pleasure which their nature is capable of, we are justified in ascribing to the preferred enjoyment a superiority in quality, so far outweighing quantity as to render it, in comparison, of small account.

Now it is an unquestionable fact that those who are equally acquainted with, and equally capable of appreciating and enjoying, both, do give a most marked preference to the manner of existence which employs their higher faculties. Few human creatures would consent to be changed into any of the lower animals, for a promise of the fullest allowance of a beast's pleasures; no intelligent human being would consent to be a fool, no instructed person would be an ignoramus, no person of feeling and conscience would be selfish and base, even though they should be persuaded that the fool, the dunce, or the rascal is better satisfied with his lot than they are with theirs. They would not resign what they possess more than he for the most complete satisfaction of all the desires which they have in common with him. If they ever fancy they would, it is only in cases of unhappiness so extreme, that to escape from it they would exchange their lot for almost any other, however undesirable in their own eyes. A being of higher faculties requires more to make him happy, is capable probably of more acute suffering, and certainly accessible to it at more points, than one of an inferior type; but in spite of these liabilities, he can never really wish to sink into what he feels to be a lower grade of existence. We may give what explanation we please of this unwillingness; we may attribute it to pride, a name which is given indiscriminately to some of the most and to some of the least estimable feelings of which mankind are capable: we may refer it to the love of liberty and personal independence, an appeal to which was with the Stoics one of the most effective means for the inculcation of it; to the love of power, or to the love of excitement, both of which do really enter into and contribute to it: but its most appropriate appellation is a sense of dignity, which all human beings possess in one form or other, and in some, though by no means in exact, proportion to their higher faculties, and which is so essential a part of the happiness of those in whom it is strong, that nothing which conflicts with it could be, otherwise than momentarily, an object of desire to them. Whoever supposes that this preference takes place at a sacrifice of happiness—that the superior being, in anything like equal circumstances, is not happier than the inferior—confounds the two very different ideas, of happiness, and content. It is indisputable that the being whose capacities of enjoyment are low, has the greatest chance of having them fully satisfied; and a highly endowed being will always feel that any happiness which he can look for, as the world is constituted, is imperfect. But he can learn to bear its imperfections, if they are at all bearable; and they will not make him envy the being who is indeed unconscious of the imperfections, but only because he feels not at all the good which those imperfections qualify. It is better to be a human being dissatisfied than a pig satisfied; better to be Socrates dissatisfied than a fool satisfied. And if the fool, or the pig, are of a different opinion, it is because they only know their own side of the question. The other party to the comparison knows both sides.

It may be objected, that many who are capable of the higher pleasures, occasionally, under the influence of temptation, postpone them to the lower. But this is quite compatible with a full appreciation of the intrinsic superiority of the higher. Men often, from infirmity of character, make their election for[1] the nearer good, though they know it to be the less valuable; and this no less when the choice is between two bodily pleasures, than when it is between bodily and mental. They pursue sensual indulgences to the injury of health, though perfectly aware that health is the greater good.

It may be further objected, that many who begin with youthful enthusiasm for everything noble, as they advance in years sink into indolence and selfishness. But I do not believe that those who undergo this very common change, voluntarily choose the lower description of pleasures in preference to the higher. I believe that before they devote themselves exclusively to the one, they have already become incapable of the other. Capacity for the nobler feelings is in most natures a very tender plant, easily killed, not only by hostile influences, but by mere want of sustenance; and in the majority of young persons it speedily dies away if the occupations to which their position in life has devoted them, and the society into which it has thrown them, are not favourable to keeping that higher capacity in exercise. Men lose their high aspirations as they lose their intellectual tastes, because they have not time or opportunity for indulging them; and they addict themselves to inferior pleasures, not because they deliberately prefer them, but because they are either the only ones to which they have access, or the only ones which they are any longer capable of enjoying. It may be questioned whether any one who has remained equally susceptible to both classes of pleasures, ever knowingly and calmly preferred the lower; though many, in all ages, have broken down in an ineffectual attempt to combine both.

---

1 Choose.

From this verdict of the only competent judges, I apprehend there can be no appeal. On a question which is the best worth having of two pleasures, or which of two modes of existence is the most grateful to the feelings, apart from its moral attributes and from its consequences, the judgment of those who are qualified by knowledge of both, or, if they differ, that of the majority among them, must be admitted as final. And there needs be the less hesitation to accept this judgment respecting the quality of pleasures, since there is no other tribunal to be referred to even on the question of quantity. What means are there of determining which is the acutest of two pains, or the intensest of two pleasurable sensations, except the general suffrage[1] of those who are familiar with both? Neither pains nor pleasures are homogeneous, and pain is always heterogeneous with pleasure. What is there to decide whether a particular pleasure is worth purchasing at the cost of a particular pain, except the feelings and judgment of the experienced? When, therefore, those feelings and judgment declare the pleasures derived from the higher faculties to be preferable *in kind*, apart from the question of intensity, to those of which the animal nature, disjoined from the higher faculties, is susceptible, they are entitled on this subject to the same regard.

I have dwelt on this point, as being a necessary part of a perfectly just conception of Utility or Happiness, considered as the directive rule of human conduct. But it is by no means an indispensable condition to the acceptance of the utilitarian standard; for that standard is not the agent's own greatest happiness, but the greatest amount of happiness altogether; and if it may possibly be doubted whether a noble character is always the happier for its nobleness, there can be no doubt that it makes other people happier, and that the world in general is immensely a gainer by it. Utilitarianism, therefore, could only attain its end by the general cultivation of nobleness of character, even if each individual were only benefited by the nobleness of others, and his own, so far as happiness is concerned, were a sheer deduction[2] from the benefit. But the bare enunciation of such an absurdity as this last, renders refutation superfluous.

According to the Greatest Happiness Principle, as above explained, the ultimate end, with reference to and for the sake of which all other things are desirable (whether we are considering our own good or that of other people), is an existence exempt as far as possible from pain, and as rich as possible in enjoyments, both in point of quantity and quality; the test of quality, and the rule for measuring it against quan-

maximise happiness for the greatest number of people

---

1   A view expressed by voting (or the right to make such a vote).
2   Subtraction (as opposed to an inference).

tity, being the preference felt by those who in their opportunities of experience, to which must be added their habits of self-consciousness and self-observation, are best furnished with the means of comparison. This, being, according to the utilitarian opinion, the end of human action, is necessarily also the standard of morality; which may accordingly be defined, the rules and precepts for human conduct, by the observance of which an existence such as has been described might be, to the greatest extent possible, secured to all mankind; and not to them only, but, so far as the nature of things admits, to the whole sentient creation.[1]

Against this doctrine, however, arises another class of objectors, who say that happiness, in any form, cannot be the rational purpose of human life and action; because, in the first place, it is unattainable: and they contemptuously ask, what right hast thou to be happy? a question which Mr. Carlyle[2] clenches by the addition, What right, a short time ago, hadst thou even *to be*? Next, they say, that men can do without happiness; that all noble human beings have felt this, and could not have become noble but by learning the lesson of Entsagen,[3] or renunciation; which lesson, thoroughly learnt and submitted to, they affirm to be the beginning and necessary condition of all virtue.

The first of these objections would go to the root of the matter were it well founded; for if no happiness is to be had at all by human beings, the attainment of it cannot be the end of morality, or of any rational conduct. Though, even in that case, something might still be said for the utilitarian theory; since utility includes not solely the pursuit of happiness, but the prevention or mitigation of unhappiness; and if the former aim be chimerical,[4] there will be all the greater scope and more imperative need for the latter, so long at least as mankind think fit to live, and do not take refuge in the simultaneous act of suicide recom-

---

1   To all creatures capable of sensation (and thus of feeling pleasure and pain).

2   Thomas Carlyle (1795–1881) was a popular Scottish writer and (somewhat reactionary) social critic. This quotation is from his 1836 book *Sartor Resartus*. As a young man Mill was heavily influenced by Carlyle's allegiance to German Romanticism, but once Carlyle began to realize that Mill did not see himself as one of his disciples, their relationship took a sharp turn for the worse. (The fact that Mill's maid accidentally used the only manuscript copy of Carlyle's *History of the French Revolution* to light a fire when Carlyle was visiting him—forcing Carlyle to rewrite all of Volume I—cannot have helped.) *Utilitarianism* is largely intended as a response to criticisms of Mill's moral theories leveled by Carlyle and others.

3   German for "to renounce or abjure." The idea it is supposed to capture is that moral behavior must be painful or difficult to be genuinely virtuous.

4   Unrealistic, fanciful.

mended under certain conditions by Novalis.[1] When, however, it is thus positively asserted to be impossible that human life should be happy, the assertion, if not something like a verbal quibble, is at least an exaggeration. If by happiness be meant a continuity of highly pleasurable excitement, it is evident enough that this is impossible. A state of exalted pleasure lasts only moments, or in some cases, and with some intermissions, hours or days, and is the occasional brilliant flash of enjoyment, not its permanent and steady flame. Of this the philosophers who have taught that happiness is the end of life were as fully aware as those who taunt them. The happiness which they meant was not a life of rapture; but moments of such, in an existence made up of few and transitory pains, many and various pleasures, with a decided predominance of the active over the passive, and having as the foundation of the whole, not to expect more from life than it is capable of bestowing. A life thus composed, to those who have been fortunate enough to obtain it, has always appeared worthy of the name of happiness. And such an existence is even now the lot of many, during some considerable portion of their lives. The present wretched education, and wretched social arrangements, are the only real hindrance to its being attainable by almost all.

The objectors perhaps may doubt whether human beings, if taught to consider happiness as the end of life, would be satisfied with such a moderate share of it. But great numbers of mankind have been satisfied with much less. The main constituents of a satisfied life appear to be two, either of which by itself is often found sufficient for the purpose: tranquillity, and excitement. With much tranquillity, many find that they can be content with very little pleasure: with much excitement, many can reconcile themselves to a considerable quantity of pain. There is assuredly no inherent impossibility in enabling even the mass of mankind to unite both; since the two are so far from being incompatible that they are in natural alliance, the prolongation of either being a preparation for, and exciting a wish for, the other. It is only those in whom indolence amounts to a vice, that do not desire excitement after an interval of repose: it is only those in whom the need of excitement is a disease, that feel the tranquillity which follows excitement dull and insipid, instead of pleasurable in direct proportion to the excitement which preceded it. When people who are tolerably for-

---

1   Novalis was the pseudonym of an early German poet and philosopher in the "Romantic" movement, Friedrich von Hardenberg (1772–1801). His most famous poem, "Hymns to the Night," was written after the death of his young fiancée from tuberculosis in 1799. Just months after its publication, von Hardenberg also succumbed to the disease.

tunate in their outward lot do not find in life sufficient enjoyment to make it valuable to them, the cause generally is, caring for nobody but themselves. To those who have neither public nor private affections, the excitements of life are much curtailed, and in any case dwindle in value as the time approaches when all selfish interests must be terminated by death: while those who leave after them objects of personal affection, and especially those who have also cultivated a fellow-feeling with the collective interests of mankind, retain as lively an interest in life on the eve of death as in the vigour of youth and health. Next to selfishness, the principal cause which makes life unsatisfactory is want[1] of mental cultivation. A cultivated mind—I do not mean that of a philosopher, but any mind to which the fountains of knowledge have been opened, and which has been taught, in any tolerable degree, to exercise its faculties—finds sources of inexhaustible interest in all that surrounds it; in the objects of nature, the achievements of art, the imaginations of poetry, the incidents of history, the ways of mankind, past and present, and their prospects in the future. It is possible, indeed, to become indifferent to all this, and that too without having exhausted a thousandth part of it; but only when one has had from the beginning no moral or human interest in these things, and has sought in them only the gratification of curiosity.

Now there is absolutely no reason in the nature of things why an amount of mental culture sufficient to give an intelligent interest in these objects of contemplation, should not be the inheritance of every one born in a civilised country. As little is there an inherent necessity that any human being should be a selfish egotist, devoid of every feeling or care but those which centre in his own miserable individuality. Something far superior to this is sufficiently common even now, to give ample earnest of what the human species may be made. Genuine private affections and a sincere interest in the public good, are possible, though in unequal degrees, to every rightly brought up human being. In a world in which there is so much to interest, so much to enjoy, and so much also to correct and improve, every one who has this moderate amount of moral and intellectual requisites is capable of an existence which may be called enviable; and unless such a person, through bad laws, or subjection to the will of others, is denied the liberty to use the sources of happiness within his reach, he will not fail to find this enviable existence, if he escape the positive evils of life, the great sources of physical and mental suffering—such as indigence, disease, and the unkindness, worthlessness, or premature loss of objects of affection. The main stress of the problem lies, therefore, in the

---

1   Lack.

contest with these calamities, from which it is a rare good fortune entirely to escape; which, as things now are, cannot be obviated, and
often cannot be in any material degree mitigated. Yet no one whose
opinion deserves a moment's consideration can doubt that most of the
great positive evils of the world are in themselves removable, and will,
if human affairs continue to improve, be in the end reduced within nar-
row limits. Poverty, in any sense implying suffering, may be completely extinguished by the wisdom of society, combined with the good
sense and providence of individuals. Even that most intractable of enemies, disease, may be indefinitely reduced in dimensions by good
physical and moral education, and proper control of noxious influences; while the progress of science holds out a promise for the future
of still more direct conquests over this detestable foe. And every advance in that direction relieves us from some, not only of the chances
which cut short our own lives, but, what concerns us still more, which
deprive us of those in whom our happiness is wrapt up.[1] As for vicis-
situdes of fortune, and other disappointments connected with worldly
circumstances, these are principally the effect either of gross impru-
dence, of ill-regulated desires, or of bad or imperfect social institutions. All the grand sources, in short, of human suffering are in a great
degree, many of them almost entirely, conquerable by human care and
effort; and though their removal is grievously slow—though a long
succession of generations will perish in the breach before the conquest
is completed, and this world becomes all that, if will and knowledge
were not wanting, it might easily be made—yet every mind sufficiently intelligent and generous to bear a part, however small and un-
conspicuous, in the endeavour, will draw a noble enjoyment from the
contest itself, which he would not for any bribe in the form of selfish
indulgence consent to be without.

And this leads to the true estimation of what is said by the objectors concerning the possibility, and the obligation, of learning to do
without happiness. Unquestionably it is possible to do without happiness; it is done involuntarily by nineteen-twentieths of mankind, even
in those parts of our present world which are least deep in barbarism;
and it often has to be done voluntarily by the hero or the martyr, for the
sake of something which he prizes more than his individual happiness.
But this something, what is it, unless the happiness of others or some
of the requisites of happiness? It is noble to be capable of resigning entirely one's own portion of happiness, or chances of it: but, after all,
this self-sacrifice must be for some end; it is not its own end; and if we

---

1   For example, Mill's wife Harriet Taylor, who died of "pulmonary congestion" in
1858.

are told that its end is not happiness, but virtue, which is better than happiness, I ask, would the sacrifice be made if the hero or martyr did not believe that it would earn for others immunity from similar sacrifices? Would it be made if he thought that his renunciation of happiness for himself would produce no fruit for any of his fellow creatures, but to make their lot like his, and place them also in the condition of persons who have renounced happiness? All honour to those who can abnegate for themselves the personal enjoyment of life, when by such renunciation they contribute worthily to increase the amount of happiness in the world; but he who does it, or professes to do it, for any other purpose, is no more deserving of admiration than the ascetic mounted on his pillar.[1] He may be an inspiriting proof of what men *can* do, but assuredly not an example of what they *should*.

Though it is only in a very imperfect state of the world's arrangements that any one can best serve the happiness of others by the absolute sacrifice of his own, yet so long as the world is in that imperfect state, I fully acknowledge that the readiness to make such a sacrifice is the highest virtue which can be found in man. I will add, that in this condition of the world, paradoxical as the assertion may be, the conscious ability to do without happiness gives the best prospect of realising such happiness as is attainable. For nothing except that consciousness can raise a person above the chances of life, by making him feel that, let fate and fortune do their worst, they have not power to subdue him: which, once felt, frees him from excess of anxiety concerning the evils of life, and enables him, like many a Stoic in the worst times of the Roman Empire,[2] to cultivate in tranquillity the sources of satisfaction accessible to him, without concerning himself about the uncertainty of their duration, any more than about their inevitable end.

Meanwhile, let utilitarians never cease to claim the morality of self-devotion as a possession which belongs by as good a right to them, as either to the Stoic or to the Transcendentalist.[3] The utilitarian morality does recognise in human beings the power of sacrificing their own greatest good for the good of others. It only refuses to admit that the sacrifice is itself a good. A sacrifice which does not increase, or tend to increase, the sum total of happiness, it considers as wasted. The only self-renunciation which it applauds, is devotion to the happiness, or

---

1 Mill is probably thinking of St. Simeon Stylites (c. 390–459), a Syrian ascetic who spent more than 30 years living at the top of various pillars, the highest of which was 20 meters tall.

2 Many Stoics were punished or killed for opposition to dictatorial Roman emperors.

3 Those—such as Kant—who think the evidence for moral truths "transcends" human sense experience.

to some of the means of happiness, of others; either of mankind collectively, or of individuals within the limits imposed by the collective interests of mankind.

I must again repeat, what the assailants of utilitarianism seldom have the justice to acknowledge, that the happiness which forms the utilitarian standard of what is right in conduct, is not the agent's own happiness, but that of all concerned. As between his own happiness and that of others, utilitarianism requires him to be as strictly impartial as a disinterested[1] and benevolent spectator. In the golden rule of Jesus of Nazareth, we read the complete spirit of the ethics of utility. To do as you would be done by, and to love your neighbour as yourself, constitute the ideal perfection of utilitarian morality. As the means of making the nearest approach to this ideal, utility would enjoin, first, that laws and social arrangements should place the happiness, or (as speaking practically it may be called) the interest, of every individual, as nearly as possible in harmony with the interest of the whole; and secondly, that education and opinion, which have so vast a power over human character, should so use that power as to establish in the mind of every individual an indissoluble association between his own happiness and the good of the whole; especially between his own happiness and the practice of such modes of conduct, negative and positive, as regard for the universal happiness prescribes; so that not only he may be unable to conceive the possibility of happiness to himself, consistently with conduct opposed to the general good, but also that a direct impulse to promote the general good may be in every individual one of the habitual motives of action, and the sentiments connected therewith may fill a large and prominent place in every human being's sentient existence. If the impugners of the utilitarian morality represented it to their own minds in this, its true character, I know not what recommendation possessed by any other morality they could possibly affirm to be wanting to it; what more beautiful or more exalted developments of human nature any other ethical system can be supposed to foster, or what springs of action, not accessible to the utilitarian, such systems rely on for giving effect to their mandates.

The objectors to utilitarianism cannot always be charged with representing it in a discreditable light. On the contrary, those among them who entertain anything like a just idea of its disinterested character, sometimes find fault with its standard as being too high for humanity. They say it is exacting too much to require that people shall always act from the inducement of promoting the general interests of society. But this is to mistake the very meaning of a standard of morals, and con-

---

1   Free from bias or self-interest (not *un*interested or bored!).

found the rule of action with the motive of it. It is the business of ethics to tell us what are our duties, or by what test we may know them; but no system of ethics requires that the sole motive of all we do shall be a feeling of duty; on the contrary, ninety-nine hundredths of all our actions are done from other motives, and rightly so done, if the rule of duty does not condemn them. It is the more unjust to utilitarianism that this particular misapprehension should be made a ground of objection to it, inasmuch as utilitarian moralists have gone beyond almost all others in affirming that the motive has nothing to do with the morality of the action, though much with the worth of the agent. He who saves a fellow creature from drowning does what is morally right, whether his motive be duty, or the hope of being paid for his trouble; he who betrays the friend that trusts him, is guilty of a crime, even if his object be to serve another friend to whom he is under greater obligations.[1]

But to speak only of actions done from the motive of duty, and in direct obedience to principle: it is a misapprehension of the utilitarian

---

1   [Mill's note:] An opponent, whose intellectual and moral fairness it is a pleasure to acknowledge (the Rev. J. Llewellyn Davies), has objected to this passage, saying, "Surely the rightness or wrongness of saving a man from drowning does depend very much upon the motive with which it is done. Suppose that a tyrant, when his enemy jumped into the sea to escape from him, saved him from drowning simply in order that he might inflict upon him more exquisite tortures, would it tend to clearness to speak of that action as 'a morally right action'? Or suppose again, according to one of the stock illustrations of ethical inquiries, that a man betrayed a trust received from a friend, because the discharge of it would fatally injure that friend himself or some one belonging to him, would utilitarianism compel one to call the betrayal 'a crime' as much as if it had been done from the meanest motive?"

I submit, that he who saves another from drowning in order to kill him by torture afterwards, does not differ only in motive from him who does the same thing from duty or benevolence; the act itself is different. The rescue of the man is, in the case supposed, only the necessary first step of an act far more atrocious than leaving him to drown would have been. Had Mr. Davies said, "the rightness or wrongness of saving a man from drowning does depend very much"—not upon the motive but—"upon the *intention*," no utilitarian would have differed from him. Mr. Davies, by an oversight too common not to be quite venial, has in this case confounded the very different ideas of Motive and Intention. There is no point at which utilitarian thinkers (and Bentham pre-eminently) have taken more pains to illustrate than this. The morality of the action depends entirely upon the intention—that is, upon what the agent *wills to do*. But the motive, that is, the feeling which makes him will to do so, when it makes no difference to the act, makes none in the morality: though it makes a great difference in our moral estimation of the agent, especially if it indicates a good or a bad habitual *disposition*—a bent of character from which useful, or from which hurtful actions are likely to arise.

mode of thought, to conceive it as implying that people should fix their minds upon so wide a generality as the world, or society at large. The great majority of good actions are intended not for the benefit of the world, but for that of individuals, of which the good of the world is made up; and the thoughts of the most virtuous man need not on these occasions travel beyond the particular persons concerned, except so far as is necessary to assure himself that in benefiting them he is not violating the rights—that is, the legitimate and authorised expectations—of any one else. The multiplication of happiness is, according to the utilitarian ethics, the object of virtue: the occasions on which any person (except one in a thousand) has it in his power to do this on an extended scale, in other words to be a public benefactor, are but exceptional; and on these occasions alone is he called on to consider public utility; in every other case, private utility, the interest or happiness of some few persons, is all he has to attend to. Those alone the influence of whose actions extends to society in general, need concern themselves habitually about so large an object. In the case of abstinences indeed—of things which people forbear to do from moral considerations, though the consequences in the particular case might be beneficial—it would be unworthy of an intelligent agent not to be consciously aware that the action is of a class which, if practised generally, would be generally injurious, and that this is the ground of the obligation to abstain from it. The amount of regard for the public interest implied in this recognition, is no greater than is demanded by every system of morals, for they all enjoin to abstain from whatever is manifestly pernicious to society.

The same considerations dispose of another reproach against the doctrine of utility, founded on a still grosser misconception of the purpose of a standard of morality, and of the very meaning of the words right and wrong. It is often affirmed[1] that utilitarianism renders men cold and unsympathising; that it chills their moral feelings towards individuals; that it makes them regard only the dry and hard consideration of the consequences of actions, not taking into their moral estimate the qualities from which those actions emanate. If the assertion means that they do not allow their judgment respecting the rightness or wrongness of an action to be influenced by their opinion of the qualities of the person who does it, this is a complaint not against utilitarianism, but against having any standard of morality at all; for certainly no known ethical standard decides an action to be good or bad because it is done by a good or a bad man, still less because done by an ami-

---

1   For example, in Charles Dickens's novel *Hard Times* (1854), especially through the character of Gradgrind.

able, a brave, or a benevolent man, or the contrary. These considerations are relevant, not to the estimation of actions, but of persons; and there is nothing in the utilitarian theory inconsistent with the fact that there are other things which interest us in persons besides the rightness and wrongness of their actions. The Stoics, indeed, with the paradoxical misuse of language which was part of their system, and by which they strove to raise themselves above all concern about anything but virtue, were fond of saying that he who has that has everything; that he, and only he, is rich, is beautiful, is a king. But no claim of this description is made for the virtuous man by the utilitarian doctrine. Utilitarians are quite aware that there are other desirable possessions and qualities besides virtue, and are perfectly willing to allow to all of them their full worth. They are also aware that a right action does not necessarily indicate a virtuous character, and that actions which are blameable, often proceed from qualities entitled to praise. When this is apparent in any particular case, it modifies their estimation, not certainly of the act, but of the agent. I grant that they are, notwithstanding, of opinion, that in the long run the best proof of a good character is good actions; and resolutely refuse to consider any mental disposition as good, of which the predominant tendency is to produce bad conduct. This makes them unpopular with many people; but it is an unpopularity which they must share with every one who regards the distinction between right and wrong in a serious light; and the reproach is not one which a conscientious utilitarian need be anxious to repel.

If no more be meant by the objection than that many utilitarians look on the morality of actions, as measured by the utilitarian standard, with too exclusive a regard, and do not lay sufficient stress upon the other beauties of character which go towards making a human being lovable or admirable, this may be admitted. Utilitarians who have cultivated their moral feelings, but not their sympathies nor their artistic perceptions, do fall into this mistake; and so do all other moralists under the same conditions. What can be said in excuse for other moralists is equally available for them, namely, that, if there is to be any error, it is better that it should be on that side. As a matter of fact, we may affirm that among utilitarians as among adherents of other systems, there is every imaginable degree of rigidity and of laxity in the application of their standard: some are even puritanically rigorous, while others are as indulgent as can possibly be desired by sinner or by sentimentalist. But on the whole, a doctrine which brings prominently forward the interest that mankind have in the repression and prevention of conduct which violates the moral law, is likely to be inferior to no other in turning the sanctions of opinion again such violations. It is true, the question, What does violate the moral law? is one on which those who recognise different standards of morality are likely now and then to differ. But difference of opinion on moral questions was not first introduced into the world by utilitarianism, while that doctrine does supply, if not always an easy, at all events a tangible and intelligible mode of deciding such differences.

∞

It may not be superfluous to notice a few more of the common misapprehensions of utilitarian ethics, even those which are so obvious and gross that it might appear impossible for any person of candour and intelligence to fall into them; since persons, even of considerable mental endowments, often give themselves so little trouble to understand the bearings of any opinion against which they entertain a prejudice, and men are in general so little conscious of this voluntary ignorance as a defect, that the vulgarest misunderstandings of ethical doctrines are continually met with in the deliberate writings of persons of the greatest pretensions both to high principle and to philosophy. We not uncommonly hear the doctrine of utility inveighed against as a *godless* doctrine. If it be necessary to say anything at all against so mere an assumption, we may say that the question depends upon what idea we have formed of the moral character of the Deity. If it be a true belief that God desires, above all things, the happiness of his creatures, and that this was his purpose in their creation, utility is not only not a godless doctrine, but more profoundly religious than any other. If it be meant that utilitarianism does not recognise the revealed will of God as the supreme law of morals, I answer, that a utilitarian who believes in the perfect goodness and wisdom of God, necessarily believes that whatever God has thought fit to reveal on the subject of morals, must fulfil the requirements of utility in a supreme degree. But others besides utilitarians have been of the opinion that the Christian revelation was intended, and is fitted, to inform the hearts and minds of mankind with a spirit which should enable them to find for themselves what is right, and incline them to do it when found, rather than to tell them, except in a very general way, what it is; and that we need a doctrine of ethics, carefully followed out, to *interpret* to us the will of God. Whether this opinion is correct or not, it is superfluous here to discuss; since whatever aid religion, either natural or revealed, can afford to ethical investigation, is as open to the utilitarian moralist as to any other. He can use it as the testimony of God to the usefulness or hurtfulness of any given course of action, by as good a right as others can use it for the indication of a transcendental law, having no connection with usefulness or with happiness.

Again, Utility is often summarily stigmatised as an immoral doctrine by giving it the name of Expediency, and taking advantage of the popular use of that term to contrast it with Principle. But the Expedient, in the sense in which it is opposed to the Right, generally means that which is expedient for the particular interest of the agent himself; as when a minister sacrifices the interests of his country to keep himself in place. When it means anything better than this, it means that which is expedient for some immediate object, some temporary purpose, but which violates a rule whose observance is expedient in a much higher degree. The Expedient, in this sense, instead of being the same thing with the useful, is a branch of the hurtful. Thus, it would often be expedient, for the purpose of getting over some momentary embarrassment, or attaining some object immediately useful to ourselves or others, to tell a lie. But inasmuch as the cultivation in ourselves of a sensitive feeling on the subject of veracity, is one of the most useful, and the enfeeblement of that feeling one of the most hurtful, things to which our conduct can be instrumental; and inasmuch as any, even unintentional, deviation from truth, does that much towards weakening the trustworthiness of human assertion, which is not only the principal support of all present social well-being, but the insufficiency of which does more than any one thing that can be named to keep back civilisation, virtue, everything on which human happiness on the largest scale depends; we feel that the violation, for a present advantage, of a rule of such transcendent expediency, is not expedient, and that he who, for the sake of a convenience to himself or to some other individual, does what depends on him to deprive mankind of the good, and inflict upon them the evil, involved in the greater or less reliance which they can place in each other's word, acts the part of one of their worst enemies. Yet that even this rule, sacred as it is, admits of possible exceptions, is acknowledged by all moralists; the chief of which is when the withholding of some fact (as of information from a malefactor, or of bad news from a person dangerously ill) would save an individual (especially an individual other than oneself) from great and unmerited evil, and when the withholding can only be effected by denial. But in order that the exception may not extend itself beyond the need, and may have the least possible effect in weakening reliance on veracity, it ought to be recognised, and, if possible, its limits defined; and if the principle of utility is good for anything, it must be good for weighing these conflicting utilities against one another, and marking out the region within which one or the other preponderates.

Again, defenders of utility often find themselves called upon to reply to such objections as this—that there is not time, previous to action, for calculating and weighing the effects of any line of conduct on the general happiness. This is exactly as if any one were to say that it is impossible to guide our conduct by Christianity, because there is not time, on every occasion on which anything has to be done, to read through the Old and New Testaments. The answer to the objection is, that there has been ample time, namely, the whole past duration of the human species. During all that time, mankind have been learning by experience the tendencies of actions; on which experience all the prudence, as well as all the morality of life, are dependent. People talk as if the commencement of this course of experience had hitherto been put off, and as if, at the moment when some man feels tempted to meddle with the property or life of another, he had to begin considering for the first time whether murder and theft are injurious to human happiness. Even then I do not think that he would find the question very puzzling; but, at all events, the matter is now done to his hand. It is truly a whimsical supposition that, if mankind were agreed in considering utility to be the test of morality, they would remain without any agreement as to what *is* useful, and would take no measures for having their notions on the subject taught to the young, and enforced by law and opinion. There is no difficulty in proving any ethical standard whatever to work ill, if we suppose universal idiocy to be conjoined with it; but on any hypothesis short of that, mankind must by this time have acquired positive beliefs as to the effects of some actions on their happiness; and the beliefs which have thus come down are the rules of morality for the multitude, and for the philosopher until he has succeeded in finding better. That philosophers might easily do this, even now, on many subjects; that the received code of ethics is by no means of divine right; and that mankind have still much to learn as to the effects of actions on the general happiness, I admit, or rather, earnestly maintain. The corollaries from the principle of utility, like the precepts of every practical art, admit of indefinite improvement, and, in a progressive state of the human mind, their improvement is perpetually going on. But to consider the rules of morality as improvable, is one thing; to pass over the intermediate generalisations entirely, and endeavour to test each individual action directly by the first principle, is another. It is a strange notion that the acknowledgment of a first principle is inconsistent with the admission of secondary ones. To inform a traveller respecting the place of his ultimate destination, is not to forbid the use of landmarks and direction-posts on the way. The proposition that happiness is the end and aim of morality, does not mean that no road ought to be laid down to that goal, or that persons going thither should not be advised to take one direction rather than another. Men really ought to leave off talking a kind of nonsense on this subject, which they would neither talk nor listen to on other matters of practical concernment. Nobody argues that the art of navigation is not founded on astronomy, because sailors cannot wait to calculate the Nautical Almanack.[1] Being rational creatures, they go to sea with it ready calculated; and all rational creatures go out upon the sea of life with their minds made up on the common questions of right and wrong, as well as on many of the far more difficult questions of wise and foolish. And this, as long as foresight is a human quality, it is to be presumed they will continue to do. Whatever we adopt as the fundamental principle of morality, we require subordinate principles to apply it by; the impossibility of doing without them, being common to all systems, can afford no argument against any one in particular; but gravely to argue as if no such secondary principles could be had, and as if mankind had remained till now, and always must remain, without drawing any general conclusions from the experience of human life, is as high a pitch, I think, as absurdity has ever reached in philosophical controversy.

The remainder of the stock arguments against utilitarianism mostly consist in laying to its charge the common infirmities of human nature, and the general difficulties which embarrass conscientious persons in shaping their course through life. We are told that a utilitarian will be apt to make his own particular case an exception to moral rules, and, when under temptation, will see a utility in the breach of a rule, greater than he will see in its observance. But is utility the only creed which is able to furnish us with excuses for evil doing, and means of cheating our own conscience? They are afforded in abundance by all doctrines which recognise as a fact in morals the existence of conflicting considerations; which all doctrines do, that have been believed by sane persons. It is not the fault of any creed, but of the complicated nature of human affairs, that rules of conduct cannot be so framed as to require no exceptions, and that hardly any kind of action can safely be laid down as either always obligatory or always condemnable. There is no ethical creed which does not temper the rigidity of its laws, by giving a certain latitude, under the moral responsibility of the agent, for accommodation to peculiarities of circumstances; and under every creed, at the opening thus made, self-deception and dishonest casuistry[2] get in. There exists no moral system under which there do not

---

1   An annual government publication that tabulates the astronomical data required for maritime navigation. (For example, the almanac might give the coordinates of the constellation Orion as it would be seen at the horizon on a particular date from various places on the earth's surface: observation of Orion at certain coordinates on that date will therefore tell you where you are.)

2   Unsound and deceptive reasoning; or, reasoning from particular cases rather than general rules.

➤ arise unequivocal cases of conflicting obligation. These are the real
difficulties, the knotty points both in the theory of ethics, and in the
conscientious guidance of personal conduct. They are overcome practically, with greater or with less success, according to the intellect and
virtue of the individual; but it can hardly be pretended that any one
will be the less qualified for dealing with them, from possessing an
ultimate standard to which conflicting rights and duties can be referred.
If utility is the ultimate source of moral obligations, utility may be in-
voked to decide between them when their demands are incompatible.
Though the application of the standard may be difficult, it is better
than none at all: while in other systems, the moral laws all claiming independent authority, there is no common umpire entitled to interfere
between them; their claims to precedence one over another rest on little better than sophistry,[1] and unless determined, as they generally are,
by the unacknowledged influence of considerations of utility, afford a
free scope for the action of personal desires and partialities. We must
remember that only in these cases of conflict between secondary principles is it requisite that first principles should be appealed to. There
is no case of moral obligation in which some secondary principle is not
involved; and if only one, there can seldom be any real doubt which
one it is, in the mind of any person by whom the principle itself is
recognised.

Chapter 3: Of the Ultimate Sanction[2] of the Principle of Utility

The question is often asked, and properly so, in regard to any supposed
moral standard—What is its sanction? what are the motives to obey it?
or more specifically, what is the source of its obligation? whence does
it derive its binding force? It is a necessary part of moral philosophy
to provide the answer to this question; which, though frequently assuming the shape of an objection to the utilitarian morality, as if it had
some special applicability to that above others, really arises in regard
to all standards. It arises, in fact, whenever a person is called on to
adopt a standard, or refer morality to any basis on which he has not
been accustomed to rest it. For the customary morality, that which education and opinion have consecrated, is the only one which presents

---

1 Plausible but misleading argument.
2 "Sanction" was a technical term in eighteenth- and nineteenth-century philosophy.
   Sanctions are the *sources* of the pleasures and pains that motivate people to act.
   For example, Bentham—in his *Introduction to the Principles of Morals and Legislation*—distinguished between four different types of sanction: "physical" (e.g.,
   hunger or sexual desire), "political" (e.g., prison), "religious" (e.g., heaven and
   hell), and "moral" (e.g., social disapproval).

itself to the mind with the feeling of being *in itself* obligatory; and when a person is asked to believe that this morality *derives* its obligation from some general principle round which custom has not thrown the same halo, the assertion is to him a paradox; the supposed corollaries seem to have a more binding force than the original theorem; the superstructure seems to stand better without, than with, what is represented as its foundation. He says to himself, I feel that I am bound not to rob or murder, betray or deceive; but why am I bound to promote the general happiness? If my own happiness lies in something else, why may I not give that the preference?

If the view adopted by the utilitarian philosophy of the nature of the moral sense be correct, this difficulty will always present itself, until the influences which form moral character have taken the same hold of the principle which they have taken of some of the consequences—until, by the improvement of education, the feeling of unity with our fellow-creatures shall be (what it cannot be denied that Christ intended it to be) as deeply rooted in our character, and to our own consciousness as completely a part of our nature, as the horror of crime is in an ordinarily well brought up young person. In the meantime, however, the difficulty has no peculiar application to the doctrine of utility, but is inherent in every attempt to analyse morality and reduce it to principles; which, unless the principle is already in men's minds invested with as much sacredness as any of its applications, always seems to divest them of a part of their sanctity.

The principle of utility either has, or there is no reason why it might not have, all the sanctions which belong to any other system of morals. Those sanctions are either external or internal. Of the external sanctions it is not necessary to speak at any length. They are, the hope of favour and the fear of displeasure, from our fellow creatures or from the Ruler of the Universe, along with whatever we may have of sympathy or affection for them, or of love and awe of Him, inclining us to do his will independently of selfish consequences. There is evidently no reason why all these motives for observance should not attach themselves to the utilitarian morality, as completely and as powerfully as to any other. Indeed, those of them which refer to our fellow creatures are sure to do so, in proportion to the amount of general intelligence; for whether there be any other ground of moral obligation than the general happiness or not, men do desire happiness; and however imperfect may be their own practice, they desire and commend all conduct in others towards themselves, by which they think their happiness is promoted. With regard to the religious motive, if men believe, as most profess to do, in the goodness of God, those who think that conduciveness to the general happiness is the essence, or even only the criterion of good, must necessarily believe that it is also that which God approves. The whole force therefore of external reward and punishment, whether physical or moral, and whether proceeding from God or from our fellow men, together with all that the capacities of human nature admit of disinterested devotion to either, become available to enforce the utilitarian morality, in proportion as that morality is recognised; and the more powerfully, the more the appliances of education and general cultivation are bent to the purpose.

So far as to external sanctions. The internal sanction of duty, whatever our standard of duty may be, is one and the same—a feeling in our own mind; a pain, more or less intense, attendant on violation of duty, which in properly cultivated moral natures rises, in the more serious cases, into shrinking from it as an impossibility. This feeling, when disinterested, and connecting itself with the pure idea of duty, and not with some particular form of it, or with any of the merely accessory circumstances, is the essence of Conscience; though in that complex phenomenon as it actually exists, the simple fact is in general all encrusted over with collateral associations, derived from sympathy, from love, and still more from fear; from all the forms of religious feeling; from the recollections of childhood and of all our past life; from self-esteem, desire of the esteem of others, and occasionally even self-abasement. This extreme complication is, I apprehend, the origin of the sort of mystical character which, by a tendency of the human mind of which there are many other examples, is apt to be attributed to the idea of moral obligation, and which leads people to believe that the idea cannot possibly attach itself to any other objects than those which, by a supposed mysterious law, are found in our present experience to excite it. Its binding force, however, consists in the existence of a mass of feeling which must be broken through in order to do what violates our standard of right, and which, if we do nevertheless violate that standard, will probably have to be encountered afterwards in the form of remorse. Whatever theory we have of the nature or origin of conscience, this is what essentially constitutes it.

The ultimate sanction, therefore, of all morality (external motives apart) being a subjective feeling in our own minds, I see nothing embarrassing to those whose standard is utility, in the question, what is the sanction of that particular standard? We may answer, the same as of all other moral standards—the conscientious feelings of mankind. Undoubtedly this sanction has no binding efficacy on those who do not possess the feelings it appeals to; but neither will these persons be more obedient to any other moral principle than to the utilitarian one. On them morality of any kind has no hold but through the external sanctions. Meanwhile the feelings exist, a fact in human nature, the reality of which, and the great power with which they are capable of acting on those in whom they have been duly cultivated, are proved by experience. No reason has ever been shown why they may not be cultivated to as great intensity in connection with the utilitarian, as with any other rule of morals.

There is, I am aware, a disposition to believe that a person who sees in moral obligation a transcendental fact, an objective reality belonging to the province of "Things in themselves," is likely to be more obedient to it than one who believes it to be entirely subjective, having its seat in human consciousness only. But whatever a person's opinion may be on this point of Ontology,[1] the force he is really urged by is his own subjective feeling, and is exactly measured by its strength. No one's belief that duty is an objective reality is stronger than the belief that God is so; yet the belief in God, apart from the expectation of actual reward and punishment, only operates on conduct through, and in proportion to, the subjective religious feeling. The sanction, so far as it is disinterested, is always in the mind itself, and the notion therefore of the transcendental moralists must be, that this sanction will not exist *in* the mind unless it is believed to have its root out of the mind; and that if a person is able to say to himself, This which is restraining me, and which is called my conscience, is only a feeling in my own mind, he may possibly draw the conclusion that when the feeling ceases the obligation ceases, and that if he find the feeling inconvenient, he may disregard it, and endeavour to get rid of it. But is this danger confined to the utilitarian morality? Does the belief that moral obligation has its seat outside the mind make the feeling of it too strong to be got rid of? The fact is so far otherwise, that all moralists admit and lament the ease with which, in the generality of minds, conscience can be silenced or stifled. The question, Need I obey my conscience? is quite as often put to themselves by persons who never heard of the principle of utility, as by its adherents. Those whose conscientious feelings are so weak as to allow of their asking this question, if they answer it affirmatively, will not do so because they believe in the transcendental theory, but because of the external sanctions.

It is not necessary, for the present purpose, to decide whether the feeling of duty is innate[2] or implanted. Assuming it to be innate, it is

---

1   Ontology is the study of what exists or of the nature of "being" itself (*on* is Greek for "being"). Questions about the reality of numbers, of fictional characters, or of theoretical entities (such as quarks or genes) are ontological questions. The particular ontological question Mill has in mind here is the existence of transcendent moral laws.

2   Inborn, possessed at birth.

an open question to what objects it naturally attaches itself, for the philosophic supporters of that theory are now agreed that the intuitive perception is of principles of morality and not of the details. If there be anything innate in the matter, I see no reason why the feeling which is innate should not be that of regard to the pleasures and pains of others. If there is any principle of morals which is intuitively obligatory, I should say it must be that. If so, the intuitive ethics would coincide with the utilitarian, and there would be no further quarrel between them. Even as it is, the intuitive moralists, though they believe that there are other intuitive moral obligations, do already believe this to be one; for they unanimously hold that a large *portion* of morality turns upon the consideration due to the interests of our fellow-creatures. Therefore, if the belief in the transcendental origin of moral obligation gives any additional efficacy to the internal sanction, it appears to me that the utilitarian principle has already the benefit of it.

On the other hand, if, as is my own belief, the moral feelings are not innate, but acquired, they are not for that reason the less natural. It is natural to man to speak, to reason, to build cities, to cultivate the ground, though these are acquired faculties. The moral feelings are not indeed a part of our nature, in the sense of being in any perceptible degree present in all of us; but this, unhappily, is a fact admitted by those who believe the most strenuously in their transcendental origin. Like the other acquired capacities above referred to, the moral faculty, if not a part of our nature, is a natural outgrowth from it; capable, like them, in a certain small degree, of springing up spontaneously; and susceptible of being brought by cultivation to a high degree of development. Unhappily it is also susceptible, by a sufficient use of the external sanctions and of the force of early impressions, of being cultivated in almost any direction: so that there is hardly anything so absurd or so mischievous that it may not, by means of these influences, be made to act on the human mind with all the authority of conscience. To doubt that the same potency might be given by the same means to the principle of utility, even if it had no foundation in human nature, would be flying in the face of all experience.

But moral associations which are wholly of artificial creation, when intellectual culture goes on, yield by degrees to the dissolving force of analysis: and if the feeling of duty, when associated with utility, would appear equally arbitrary; if there were no leading department of our nature, no powerful class of sentiments, with which that association would harmonise, which would make us feel it congenial, and incline us not only to foster it in others (for which we have abundant interested motives), but also to cherish it in ourselves; if there were not, in short, a natural basis of sentiment for utilitarian morality, it might well happen that this association also, even after it had been implanted by education, might be analysed away.

But there is this basis of powerful natural sentiment; and this it is which, when once the general happiness is recognised as the ethical standard, will constitute the strength of the utilitarian morality. This firm foundation is that of the social feelings of mankind; the desire to be in unity with our fellow creatures, which is already a powerful principle in human nature, and happily one of those which tend to become stronger, even without express inculcation,[1] from the influences of advancing civilisation. The social state is at once so natural, so necessary, and so habitual to man, that, except in some unusual circumstances or by an effort of voluntary abstraction, he never conceives himself otherwise than as a member of a body; and this association is riveted more and more, as mankind are further removed from the state of savage independence. Any condition, therefore, which is essential to a state of society, becomes more and more an inseparable part of every person's conception of the state of things which he is born into, and which is the destiny of a human being. Now, society between human beings, except in the relation of master and slave, is manifestly impossible on any other footing than that the interests of all are to be consulted. Society between equals can only exist on the understanding that the interests of all are to be regarded equally. And since in all states of civilisation, every person, except an absolute monarch, has equals, every one is obliged to live on these terms with somebody; and in every age some advance is made towards a state in which it will be impossible to live permanently on other terms with anybody. In this way people grow up unable to conceive as possible to them a state of total disregard of other people's interests. They are under a necessity of conceiving themselves as at least abstaining from all the grosser injuries, and (if only for their own protection) living in a state of constant protest against them. They are also familiar with the fact of co-operating with others and proposing to themselves a collective, not an individual interest as the aim (at least for the time being) of their actions. So long as they are co-operating, their ends are identified with those of others; there is at least a temporary feeling that the interests of others are their own interests. Not only does all strengthening of social ties, and all healthy growth of society, give to each individual a stronger personal interest in practically consulting the welfare of others; it also leads him to identify his *feelings* more and more with their good, or at least with an even greater degree of practical consideration for it. He comes, as though in-

---

1   Frequent repetition or instruction, intended to firmly impress something in someone's mind.

stinctively, to be conscious of himself as a being who *of course* pays regard to others. The good of others becomes to him a thing naturally and necessarily to be attended to, like any of the physical conditions of our existence. Now, whatever amount of this feeling a person has, he is urged by the strongest motives both of interest and of sympathy to demonstrate it, and to the utmost of his power encourage it in others; and even if he has none of it himself, he is as greatly interested as any one else that others should have it. Consequently the smallest germs of the feeling are laid hold of and nourished by the contagion of sympathy and the influences of education; and a complete web of corroborative association is woven round it, by the powerful agency of the external sanctions. This mode of conceiving ourselves and human life, as civilisation goes on, is felt to be more and more natural. Every step in political improvement renders it more so, by removing the sources of opposition of interest, and levelling those inequalities of legal privilege between individuals or classes, owing to which there are large portions of mankind whose happiness it is still practicable to disregard. In an improving state of the human mind, the influences are constantly on the increase, which tend to generate in each individual a feeling of unity with all the rest; which, if perfect, would make him never think of, or desire, any beneficial condition for himself, in the benefits of which they are not included. If we now suppose this feeling of unity to be taught as a religion, and the whole force of education, of institutions, and of opinion, directed, as it once was in the case of religion, to make every person grow up from infancy surrounded on all sides both by the profession and the practice of it, I think that no one, who can realise this conception, will feel any misgiving about the sufficiency of the ultimate sanction for the Happiness morality. To any ethical student who finds the realisation difficult, I recommend, as a means of facilitating it, the second of M. Comte's two principle works, the *Système de Politique Positive*.[1] I entertain the strongest objections to the system of politics and morals set forth in that treatise; but I think it has superabundantly shown the possibility of giving to the service of humanity, even without the aid of belief in a Providence, both the psychical power and the social efficacy of a religion; making it take hold of human life, and colour all thought, feeling, and action, in a manner of which the greatest ascendancy ever exercised by any religion may be but a type and foretaste; and of which the danger is, not that it

---

1   This 1854 book by French political philosopher and sociologist Auguste Comte (1798–1857) advocated a capitalist dictatorship based on science as the ideal form of society, and urged that theistic conceptions of religion be replaced by a scientific "religion of humanity."

should be insufficient but that it should be so excessive as to interfere unduly with human freedom and individuality.

Neither is it necessary to the feeling which constitutes the binding force of the utilitarian morality on those who recognise it, to wait for those social influences which would make its obligation felt by mankind at large. In the comparatively early state of human advancement in which we now live, a person cannot indeed feel that entireness of sympathy with all others, which would make any real discordance in the general direction of their conduct in life impossible; but already a person in whom the social feeling is at all developed, cannot bring himself to think of the rest of his fellow creatures as struggling rivals with him for the means of happiness, whom he must desire to see defeated in their object in order that he may succeed in his. The deeply rooted conception which every individual even now has of himself as a social being, tends to make him feel it one of his natural wants that there should be harmony between his feelings and aims and those of his fellow creatures. If differences of opinion and of mental culture make it impossible for him to share many of their actual feelings— perhaps make him denounce and defy those feelings—he still needs to be conscious that his real aim and theirs do not conflict; that he is not opposing himself to what they really wish for, namely their own good, but is, on the contrary, promoting it. This feeling in most individuals is much inferior in strength to their selfish feelings, and is often wanting altogether. But to those who have it, it possesses all the characters of a natural feeling. It does not present itself to their minds as a superstition of education, or a law despotically imposed by the power of society, but as an attribute which it would not be well for them to be without. This conviction is the ultimate sanction of the greatest happiness morality. This it is which makes any mind, of well-developed feelings, work with, and not against, the outward motives to care for others, afforded by what I have called the external sanctions; and when those sanctions are wanting, or act in an opposite direction, constitutes in itself a powerful internal binding force, in proportion to the sensitiveness and thoughtfulness of the character; since few but those whose mind is a moral blank, could bear to lay out their course of life on the plan of paying no regard to others except so far as their own private interest compels.

Chapter 4: Of What Sort of Proof the Principle of Utility Is Susceptible

It has already been remarked, that questions of ultimate ends do not admit of proof, in the ordinary acceptation of the term. To be incapable of proof by reasoning is common to all first principles; to the first premises of our knowledge,[1] as well as to those of our conduct. But the former, being matters of fact, may be the subject of a direct appeal to the faculties which judge of fact—namely, our senses, and our internal consciousness.[2] Can an appeal be made to the same faculties on questions of practical ends? Or by what other faculty is cognisance taken of them?

Questions about ends are, in other words, questions about what things are desirable. The utilitarian doctrine is, that happiness is desirable, and the only thing desirable, as an end; all other things being only desirable as means to that end. What ought to be required of this doctrine—what conditions is it requisite that the doctrine should fulfil—to make good its claim to be believed?

The only proof capable of being given that an object is visible, is that people actually see it. The only proof that a sound is audible, is that people hear it: and so of the other sources of our experience. In like manner, I apprehend, the sole evidence it is possible to produce that anything is desirable, is that people do actually desire it. If the end which the utilitarian doctrine proposes to itself were not, in theory and in practice, acknowledged to be an end, nothing could ever convince any person that it was so. No reason can be given why the general happiness is desirable, except that each person, so far as he believes it to be attainable, desires his own happiness. This, however, being a fact, we have not only all the proof which the case admits of, but all which it is possible to require, that happiness is a good: that each person's happiness is a good to that person, and the general happiness, therefore, a good to the aggregate of all persons. Happiness has made out its title as *one* of the ends of conduct, and consequently one of the criteria of morality.

But it has not, by this alone, proved itself to be the sole criterion. To do that, it would seem, by the same rule, necessary to show, not only that people desire happiness, but that they never desire anything else. Now it is palpable that they do desire things which, in common language, are decidedly distinguished from happiness. They desire, for example, virtue, and the absence of vice, no less really than pleasure and the absence of pain. The desire of virtue is not as universal, but it is as authentic a fact, as the desire of happiness. And hence the opponents of the utilitarian standard deem that they have a right to infer that there are other ends of human action besides happiness, and that happiness is not the standard of approbation and disapprobation.

---

1 Sense experience.
2 Mill means the memory of something previously experienced.

But does the utilitarian doctrine deny that people desire virtue, or maintain that virtue is not a thing to be desired? The very reverse. It maintains not only that virtue is to be desired, but that it is to be desired disinterestedly, for itself. Whatever may be the opinion of utilitarian moralists as to the original conditions by which virtue is made virtue; however they may believe (as they do) that actions and dispositions are only virtuous because they promote another end than virtue; yet this being granted, and it having been decided, from considerations of this description, what is virtuous, they not only place virtue at the very head of the things which are good as means to the ultimate end, but they also recognise as a psychological fact the possibility of its being, to the individual, a good in itself, without looking to any end beyond it; and hold, that the mind is not in a right state, not in a state conformable to Utility, not in the state most conducive to the general happiness, unless it does love virtue in this manner—as a thing desirable in itself, even although, in the individual instance, it should not produce those other desirable consequences which it tends to produce, and on account of which it is held to be virtue. This opinion is not, in the smallest degree, a departure from the Happiness principle. The ingredients of happiness are very various, and each of them is desirable in itself, and not merely when considered as swelling an aggregate. The principle of utility does not mean that any given pleasure, as music, for instance, or any given exemption from pain, as for example health, is to be looked upon as means to a collective something termed happiness, and to be desired on that account. They are desired and desirable in and for themselves; besides being means, they are a part of the end. Virtue, according to the utilitarian doctrine, is not naturally and originally part of the end, but it is capable of becoming so; and in those who love it disinterestedly it has become so, and is desired and cherished, not as a means to happiness, but as a part of their happiness.

To illustrate this farther, we may remember that virtue is not the only thing, originally a means, and which if it were not a means· to anything else, would be and remain indifferent, but which by association with what it is a means to, comes to be desired for itself, and that too with the utmost intensity. What, for example, shall we say of the love of money? There is nothing originally more desirable about money than about any heap of glittering pebbles. Its worth is solely that of the things which it will buy; the desires for other things than itself, which it is a means of gratifying. Yet the love of money is not only one of the strongest moving forces of human life, but money is, in many cases, desired in and for itself, the desire to possess it is often stronger than the desire to use it, and goes on increasing when all the desires which point to ends beyond it, to be compassed by it, are falling off. It may, then, be said truly, that money is desired not for the sake of an end, but as part of the end. From being a means to happiness, it has come to be itself a principal ingredient of the individual's conception of happiness. The same may be said of the majority of the great objects of human life—power, for example, or fame; except that to each of these there is a certain amount of immediate pleasure annexed, which has at least the semblance of being naturally inherent in them; a thing which cannot be said of money. Still, however, the strongest natural attraction, both of power and of fame, is the immense aid they give to the attainment of our other wishes; and it is the strong association thus generated between them and all our objects of desire, which gives to the direct desire of them the intensity it often assumes, so as in some characters to surpass in strength all other desires. In these cases the means have become a part of the end, and a more important part of it than any of the things which they are means to. What was once desired as an instrument for the attainment of happiness, has come to be desired for its own sake. In being desired for its own sake it is, however, desired as *part* of happiness. The person is made, or thinks he would be made, happy by its mere possession; and is made unhappy by failure to obtain it. The desire of it is not a different thing from the desire of happiness, any more than the love of music, or the desire of health. They are included in happiness. They are some of the elements of which the desire of happiness is made up. Happiness is not an abstract idea, but a concrete whole; and these are some of its parts. And the utilitarian standard sanctions and approves their being so. Life would be a poor thing, very ill provided with sources of happiness, if there were not this provision of nature, by which things originally indifferent, but conducive to, or otherwise associated with, the satisfaction of our primitive desires, become in themselves sources of pleasure more valuable than the primitive pleasures, both in permanency, in the space of human existence that they are capable of covering, and even in intensity.

Virtue, according to the utilitarian conception, is a good of this description. There was no original desire of it, or motive to it, save its conduciveness to pleasure, and especially to protection from pain. But through the association thus formed, it may be felt a good in itself, and desired as such with as great intensity as any other good; and with this difference between it and the love of money, of power, or of fame, that all of these may, and often do, render the individual noxious to the other members of the society to which he belongs, whereas there is

nothing which makes him so much a blessing to them as the cultivation of the disinterested love of virtue. And consequently, the utilitarian standard, while it tolerates and approves those other acquired
desires, up to the point beyond which they would be more injurious to
the general happiness than promotive of it, enjoins and requires the
cultivation of the love of virtue up to the greatest strength possible, as
being above all things important to the general happiness.

It results from the preceding considerations, that there is in reality
nothing desired except happiness. Whatever is desired otherwise than
as a means to some end beyond itself, and ultimately to happiness, is
desired as itself a part of happiness, and is not desired for itself until
it has become so. Those who desire virtue for its own sake, desire it either because the consciousness of it is a pleasure, or because the consciousness of being without it is a pain, or for both reasons united; as
in truth the pleasure and pain seldom exist separately, but almost always together, the same person feeling pleasure in the degree of virtue
attained, and pain in not having attained more. If one of these gave
him no pleasure, and the other no pain, he would not love or desire
virtue, or would desire it only for the other benefits which it might
produce to himself or to persons whom he cared for.

We have now, then, an answer to the question, of what sort of proof
the principle of utility is susceptible. If the opinion which I have now
stated is psychologically true—if human nature is so constituted as to
desire nothing which is not either a part of happiness or a means of
happiness, we can have no other proof, and we require no other, that
these are the only things desirable. If so, happiness is the sole end of
human action, and the promotion of it the test by which to judge of all
human conduct; from whence it necessarily follows that it must be the
criterion of morality, since a part is included in the whole.

And now to decide whether this is really so; whether mankind do
desire nothing for itself but that which is a pleasure to them, or of
which the absence is a pain; we have evidently arrived at a question of
fact and experience, dependent, like all similar questions, upon evidence. It can only be determined by practised self-consciousness and
self-observation, assisted by observation of others. I believe that these
sources of evidence, impartially consulted, will declare that desiring a
thing and finding it pleasant, aversion to it and thinking of it as painful,
are phenomena entirely inseparable, or rather two parts of the same
phenomenon; in strictness of language, two different modes of nam-
ing the same psychological fact: that to think of an object as desirable
(unless for the sake of its consequences), and to think of it as pleasant,
are one and the same thing; and that to desire anything, except in pro-

portion as the idea of it is pleasant, is a physical and metaphysical[1] impossibility.

So obvious does this appear to me, that I expect it will hardly be disputed: and the objection made will be, not that desire can possibly be directed to anything ultimately except pleasure and exemption from pain, but that the will is a different thing from desire; that a person of confirmed virtue, or any other person whose purposes are fixed, carries out his purposes without any thought of the pleasure he has in contemplating them, or expects to derive from their fulfilment; and persists in acting on them, even though these pleasures are much diminished, by changes in his character or decay of his passive sensibilities, or are outweighed by the pains which the pursuit of the purposes may bring upon him. All this I fully admit, and have stated it elsewhere, as positively and emphatically as any one. Will, the active phenomenon, is a different thing from desire, the state of passive sensibility, and though originally an offshoot from it, may in time take root and detach itself from the parent stock; so much so, that in the case of an habitual purpose, instead of willing the thing because we desire it, we often desire it only because we will it. This, however, is but an instance of that familiar fact, the power of habit, and is nowise confined to the case of virtuous actions. Many indifferent things, which men originally did from a motive of some sort, they continue to do from habit. Sometimes this is done unconsciously, the consciousness coming only after the action: at other times with conscious volition, but volition which has become habitual, and is put in operation by the force of habit, in opposition perhaps to the deliberate preference, as often happens with those who have contracted habits of vicious or hurtful indulgence. Third and last comes the case in which the habitual act of will in the individual instance is not in contradiction to the general intention prevailing at other times, but in fulfilment of it; as in the case of the person of confirmed virtue, and of all who pursue deliberately and consistently any determinate end. The distinction between will and desire thus understood is an authentic and highly important psychological fact; but the fact consists solely in this—that will, like all other parts of our constitution, is amenable to habit, and that we may will from habit what we no longer desire for itself or desire only because we will it. It is not the less true that will, in the beginning, is entirely produced by desire; including in that term the

---

1 Mill probably means "psychological." In his view, not only do human beings actually desire things "in proportion as the idea of it is pleasant," but there is no possible human psychology that would be otherwise.

repelling influence of pain as well as the attractive one of pleasure. Let us take into consideration, no longer the person who has a confirmed will to do right, but him in whom that virtuous will is still feeble, conquerable by temptation, and not to be fully relied on; by what means can it be strengthened? How can the will to be virtuous, where it does not exist in sufficient force, be implanted or awakened? Only by making the person *desire* virtue—by making him think of it in a pleasurable light, or of its absence in a painful one. It is by associating the doing right with pleasure, or the doing wrong with pain, or by eliciting and impressing and bringing home to the person's experience the pleasure naturally involved in the one or the pain in the other, that it is possible to call forth that will to be virtuous, which, when confirmed, acts without any thought of either pleasure or pain. Will is the child of desire, and passes out of the dominion of its parent only to come under that of habit. That which is the result of habit affords no presumption of being intrinsically good; and there would be no reason for wishing that the purpose of virtue should become independent of pleasure and pain, were it not that the influence of the pleasurable and painful associations which prompt to virtue is not sufficiently to be depended on for unerring constancy of action until it has acquired the support of habit. Both in feeling and in conduct, habit is the only thing which imparts certainty; and it is because of the importance to others of being able to rely absolutely on one's feelings and conduct, and to oneself of being able to rely on one's own, that the will to do right ought to be cultivated into this habitual independence. In other words, this state of the will is a means to good, not intrinsically a good; and does not contradict the doctrine that nothing is a good to human beings but in so far as it is either itself pleasurable, or a means of attaining pleasure or averting pain.

But if this doctrine be true, the principle of utility is proved. Whether it is so or not, must now be left to the consideration of the thoughtful reader.

Chapter 5: On the Connection between Justice and Utility

In all ages of speculation, one of the strongest obstacles to the reception of the doctrine that Utility or Happiness is the criterion of right and wrong, has been drawn from the idea of justice. The powerful sentiment, and apparently clear perception, which that word recalls with a rapidity and certainty resembling an instinct, have seemed to the majority of thinkers to point to an inherent quality in things; to show that the just must have an existence in Nature as something absolute, generically distinct from every variety of the Expedient,[1] and, in idea, opposed to it, though (as is commonly acknowledged) never, in the long run, disjoined from it in fact.

In the case of this, as of our other moral sentiments, there is no necessary connection between the question of its origin, and that of its binding force. That a feeling is bestowed on us by Nature, does not necessarily legitimate all its promptings. The feeling of justice might be a peculiar instinct, and might yet require, like our other instincts, to be controlled and enlightened by a higher reason. If we have intellectual instincts, leading us to judge in a particular way, as well as animal instincts that prompt us to act in a particular way, there is no necessity that the former should be more infallible in their sphere than the latter in theirs: it may as well happen that wrong judgments are occasionally suggested by those, as wrong actions by these. But though it is one thing to believe that we have natural feelings of justice, and another to acknowledge them as an ultimate criterion of conduct, these two opinions are very closely connected in point of fact. Mankind are always predisposed to believe that any subjective feeling, not otherwise accounted for, is a revelation of some objective reality. Our present object is to determine whether the reality, to which the feeling of justice corresponds, is one which needs any such special revelation; whether the justice or injustice of an action is a thing intrinsically peculiar, and distinct from all its other qualities, or only a combination of certain of those qualities, presented under a peculiar aspect. For the purpose of this inquiry it is practically important to consider whether the feeling itself, of justice and injustice, is *sui generis*[2] like our sensations of color and taste, or a derivative feeling, formed by a combination of others. And this it is the more essential to examine, as people are in general willing enough to allow, that objectively the dictates of justice coincide with a part of the field of General Expediency; but inasmuch as the subjective mental feeling of justice is different from that which commonly attaches to simple expediency, and, except in the extreme cases of the latter, is far more imperative in its demands, people find it difficult to see, in justice, only a particular kind or branch of general utility, and think that its superior binding force requires a totally different origin.

To throw light upon this question, it is necessary to attempt to ascertain what is the distinguishing character of justice, or of injustice:

---

1   An action is "expedient" in Mill's terms when it produces utility—when, that is, it will result in the greatest happiness for the greatest number of people.

2   Latin: "of its own kind."

what is the quality, or whether there is any quality, attributed in common to all modes of conduct designated as unjust (for justice, like many other moral attributes, is best defined by its opposite), and distinguishing them from such modes of conduct as are disapproved, but without having that particular epithet of disapprobation[1] applied to them. If in everything which men are accustomed to characterize as just or unjust, some one common attribute or collection of attributes is always present, we may judge whether this particular attribute or combination of attributes would be capable of gathering round it a sentiment of that peculiar character and intensity by virtue of the general laws of our emotional constitution, or whether the sentiment is inexplicable, and requires to be regarded as a special provision of Nature. If we find the former to be the case, we shall, in resolving this question, have resolved also the main problem: if the latter, we shall have to seek for some other mode of investigating it.

∞

To find the common attributes of a variety of objects, it is necessary to begin by surveying the objects themselves in the concrete. Let us therefore advert successively[2] to the various modes of action, and arrangements of human affairs, which are classed, by universal or widely spread opinion, as Just or as Unjust. The things well known to excite the sentiments associated with those names are of a very multifarious character. I shall pass them rapidly in review, without studying any particular arrangement.

In the first place, it is mostly considered unjust to deprive any one of his personal liberty, his property, or any other thing which belongs to him by law. Here, therefore, is one instance of the application of the terms just and unjust in a perfectly definite sense, namely, that it is just to respect, unjust to violate, the *legal rights* of any one. But this judgment admits of several exceptions, arising from the other forms in which the notions of justice and injustice present themselves. For example, the person who suffers the deprivation may (as the phrase is) have *forfeited* the rights which he is so deprived of: a case to which we shall return presently. But also,

Secondly; the legal rights of which he is deprived, may be rights which *ought* not to have belonged to him; in other words, the law which confers on him these rights, may be a bad law. When it is so, or when (which is the same thing for our purpose) it is supposed to be so,

---

1   Insulting term of disapproval.
2   Refer, one-by-one, in turn.

opinions will differ as to the justice or injustice of infringing it. Some maintain that no law, however bad, ought to be disobeyed by an individual citizen; that his opposition to it, if shown at all, should only be shown in endeavoring to get it altered by competent authority. This opinion (which condemns many of the most illustrious benefactors of mankind, and would often protect pernicious institutions against the only weapons which, in the state of things existing at the time, have any chance of succeeding against them) is defended, by those who hold it, on grounds of expediency; principally on that of the importance, to the common interest of mankind, of maintaining inviolate the sentiment of submission to law. Other persons, again, hold the directly contrary opinion, that any law, judged to be bad, may blamelessly be disobeyed, even though it be not judged to be unjust, but only inexpedient; while others would confine the license of disobedience to the case of unjust laws: but again, some say, that all laws which are inexpedient are unjust; since every law imposes some restriction on the natural liberty of mankind, which restriction is an injustice, unless legitimated by tending to their good. Among these diversities of opinion, it seems to be universally admitted that there may be unjust laws, and that law, consequently, is not the ultimate criterion of justice, but may give to one person a benefit, or impose on another an evil, which justice condemns. When, however, a law is thought to be unjust, it seems always to be regarded as being so in the same way in which a breach of law is unjust, namely, by infringing somebody's right; which, as it cannot in this case be a legal right, receives a different appellation, and is called a moral right. We may say, therefore, that a second case of injustice consists in taking or withholding from any person that to which he has a *moral right*.

Thirdly, it is universally considered just that each person should obtain that (whether good or evil) which he *deserves*; and unjust that he should obtain a good, or be made to undergo an evil, which he does not deserve. This is, perhaps, the clearest and most emphatic form in which the idea of justice is conceived by the general mind. As it involves the notion of desert, the question arises, what constitutes desert? Speaking in a general way, a person is understood to deserve good if he does right, evil if he does wrong; and in a more particular sense, to deserve good from those to whom he does or has done good, and evil from those to whom he does or has done evil. The precept of returning good for evil has never been regarded as a case of the fulfillment of justice, but as one in which the claims of justice are waived, in obedience to other considerations.

Fourthly, it is confessedly unjust to *break faith* with any one: to violate an engagement, either express or implied, or disappoint expectations raised by our conduct, at least if we have raised those expectations knowingly and voluntarily. Like the other obligations of justice already spoken of, this one is not regarded as absolute, but as capable of being overruled by a stronger obligation of justice on the other side; or by such conduct on the part of the person concerned as is deemed to absolve us from our obligation to him, and to constitute a *forfeiture* of the benefit which he has been led to expect.

Fifthly, it is, by universal admission, inconsistent with justice to be *partial*; to show favor or preference to one person over another, in matters to which favor and preference do not properly apply. Impartiality, however, does not seem to be regarded as a duty in itself, but rather as instrumental to some other duty; for it is admitted that favor and preference are not always censurable, and indeed the cases in which they are condemned are rather the exception than the rule. A person would be more likely to be blamed than applauded for giving his family or friends no superiority in good offices[1] over strangers, when he could do so without violating any other duty; and no one thinks it unjust to seek one person in preference to another as a friend, connection, or companion. Impartiality where rights are concerned is of course obligatory, but this is involved in the more general obligation of giving to every one his right. A tribunal, for example, must be impartial, because it is bound to award, without regard to any other consideration, a disputed object to the one of two parties who has the right to it. There are other cases in which impartiality means, being solely influenced by desert; as with those who, in the capacity of judges, preceptors, or parents, administer reward and punishment as such. There are cases, again, in which it means, being solely influenced by consideration for the public interest; as in making a selection among candidates for a government employment. Impartiality, in short, as an obligation of justice, may be said to mean, being exclusively influenced by the considerations which it is supposed ought to influence the particular case in hand; and resisting the solicitation of any motives which prompt to conduct different from what those considerations would dictate.

Nearly allied to the idea of impartiality is that of *equality*; which often enters as a component part both into the conception of justice and into the practice of it, and, in the eyes of many persons, constitutes its essence. But in this, still more than in any other case, the notion of justice varies in different persons, and always conforms in its variations to their notion of utility. Each person maintains that equality is the dictate of justice, except where he thinks that expediency requires inequality. The justice of giving equal protection to the rights of all, is

---

1   Services, kindnesses, attentions.

maintained by those who support the most outrageous inequality in the rights themselves. Even in slave countries it is theoretically admitted that the rights of the slave, such as they are, ought to be as sacred as those of the master; and that a tribunal which fails to enforce them with equal strictness is wanting in justice; while, at the same time, institutions which leave to the slave scarcely any rights to enforce, are not deemed unjust, because they are not deemed inexpedient. Those who think that utility requires distinctions of rank, do not consider it unjust that riches and social privileges should be unequally dispensed; but those who think this inequality inexpedient, think it unjust also. Whoever thinks that government is necessary, sees no injustice in as much inequality as is constituted by giving to the magistrate powers not granted to other people. Even among those who hold leveling[1] doctrines, there are as many questions of justice as there are differences of opinion about expediency. Some Communists consider it unjust that the produce of the labor of the community should be shared on any other principle than that of exact equality; others think it just that those should receive most whose wants are greatest; while others hold that those who work harder, or who produce more, or whose services are more valuable to the community, may justly claim a larger quota in the division of the produce. And the sense of natural justice may be plausibly appealed to on behalf of every one of these opinions.

Among so many diverse applications of the term justice, which yet is not regarded as ambiguous, it is a matter of some difficulty to seize the mental link which holds them together, and on which the moral sentiment adhering to the term essentially depends. Perhaps, in this embarrassment, some help may be derived from the history of the word, as indicated by its etymology.[2]

In most, if not all, languages, the etymology of the word which corresponds to Just, points to an origin connected either with positive law or with that which was in most cases the primitive form of law—authoritative custom. *Justum* is a form of *jussum*, that which has been ordered.[3] *Jus* is of the same origin. Δίκαιον [dikaion] comes from δίκη [dikē], of which the principal meaning, at least in the historical ages of Greece, was a suit at law. Originally, indeed, it meant only the mode or *manner* of doing things, but it early came to mean the *prescribed* manner; that which the recognised authorities, patriarchal, judicial, or political, would enforce. *Recht*, from which came *right* and *righteous*, is synonymous with law. The original meaning indeed of *recht* did not

---

1   Equality-producing.
2   The study of the origins of words, and of their changes in meaning over time.
3   Mill deals in turn with Latin, Greek, and German, before turning to French.

point to law, but to physical straightness; as *wrong* and its Latin equivalents meant twisted or tortuous; and from this it is argued that right did not originally mean law, but on the contrary law meant right. But however this may be, the fact that *recht* and *droit* became restricted in their meaning to positive law, although much which is not required by law is equally necessary to moral straightness or rectitude, is as significant of the original character of moral ideas as if the derivation had been the reverse way. The courts of justice, the administration of justice, are the courts and the administration of law. *La Justice*, in French, is the established term for judicature. There can, I think, be no doubt that the *idée mère*,[1] the primitive element, in the formation of the notion of justice, was conformity to law. It constituted the entire idea among the Hebrews, up to the birth of Christianity; as might be expected in the case of a people whose laws attempted to embrace all subjects on which precepts were required, and who believed those laws to be a direct emanation from the Supreme Being. But other nations, and in particular the Greeks and Romans, who knew that their laws had been made originally, and still continued to be made, by men, were not afraid to admit that those men might make bad laws; might do, by law, the same things, and from the same motives, which if done by individuals without the sanction of law, would be called unjust. And hence the sentiment of injustice came to be attached, not to all violations of law, but only to violations of such laws as ought to exist, including such as ought to exist, but do not; and to laws themselves, if supposed to be contrary to what ought to be law. In this manner the idea of law and of its injunctions was still predominant in the notion of justice, even when the laws actually in force ceased to be accepted as the standard of it.

It is true that mankind consider the idea of justice and its obligations as applicable to many things which neither are, nor is it desired that they should be, regulated by law. Nobody desires that laws should interfere with the whole detail of private life; yet every one allows that in all daily conduct a person may and does show himself to be either just or unjust. But even here, the idea of the breach of what ought to be law, still lingers in a modified shape. It would always give us pleasure, and chime in with our feelings of fitness, that acts which we deem unjust should be punished, though we do not always think it expedient that this should be done by the tribunals. We forego that gratification on account of incidental inconveniences. We should be glad to see just conduct enforced and injustice repressed, even in the minutest details, if we were not, with reason, afraid of trusting the magistrate

---

1   Fundamental or original idea (French for "mother idea").

with so unlimited an amount of power over individuals. When we think that a person is bound in justice to do a thing, it is an ordinary form of language to say, that he ought to be compelled to do it. We should be gratified to see the obligation enforced by anybody who had the power. If we see that its enforcement by law would be inexpedient, we lament the impossibility, we consider the impunity given to injustice as an evil, and strive to make amends for it by bringing a strong expression of our own and the public disapprobation to bear upon the offender. Thus the idea of legal constraint is still the generating idea of the notion of justice, though undergoing several transformations before that notion, as it exists in an advanced state of society, becomes complete.

The above is, I think, a true account, as far as it goes, of the origin and progressive growth of the idea of justice. But we must observe, that it contains, as yet, nothing to distinguish that obligation from moral obligation in general. For the truth is, that the idea of penal sanction, which is the essence of law, enters not only into the conception of injustice, but into that of any kind of wrong. We do not call anything wrong, unless we mean to imply that a person ought to be punished in some way or other for doing it; if not by law, by the opinion of his fellow-creatures; if not by opinion, by the reproaches of his own conscience. This seems the real turning point of the distinction between morality and simple expediency. It is a part of the notion of Duty in every one of its forms, that a person may rightfully be compelled to fulfill it. Duty is a thing which may be *exacted* from a person, as one exacts a debt. Unless we think that it may be exacted from him, we do not call it his duty. Reasons of prudence, or the interest of other people, may militate against actually exacting it; but the person himself, it is clearly understood, would not be entitled to complain. There are other things, on the contrary, which we wish that people should do, which we like or admire them for doing, perhaps dislike or despise them for not doing, but yet admit that they are not bound to do; it is not a case of moral obligation; we do not blame them, that is, we do not think that they are proper objects of punishment. How we come by these ideas of deserving and not deserving punishment, will appear, perhaps, in the sequel;[1] but I think there is no doubt that this distinction lies at the bottom of the notions of right and wrong; that we call any conduct wrong, or employ, instead, some other term of dislike or disparagement, according as we think that the person ought, or ought not, to be punished for it; and we say, it would be right, to do so and so, or merely that it would be desirable or laudable, according as we

---

1   In what follows (in this work).

would wish to see the person whom it concerns, compelled, or only persuaded and exhorted, to act in that manner.[1]

This, therefore, being the characteristic difference which marks off, not justice, but morality in general, from the remaining provinces of Expediency and Worthiness; the character is still to be sought which distinguishes justice from other branches of morality. Now it is known that ethical writers divide moral duties into two classes, denoted by the ill-chosen expressions, duties of perfect and of imperfect obligation; the latter being those in which, though the act is obligatory, the particular occasions of performing it are left to our choice, as in the case of charity or beneficence, which we are indeed bound to practice, but not towards any definite person, nor at any prescribed time. In the more precise language of philosophic jurists, duties of perfect obligation are those duties in virtue of which a correlative *right* resides in some person or persons; duties of imperfect obligation are those moral obligations which do not give birth to any right. I think it will be found that this distinction exactly coincides with that which exists between justice and the other obligations of morality. In our survey of the various popular acceptations of justice, the term appeared generally to involve the idea of a personal right—a claim on the part of one or more individuals, like that which the law gives when it confers a proprietary or other legal right. Whether the injustice consists in depriving a person of a possession, or in breaking faith with him, or in treating him worse than he deserves, or worse than other people who have no greater claims, in each case the supposition implies two things—a wrong done, and some assignable person who is wronged. Injustice may also be done by treating a person better than others; but the wrong in this case is to his competitors, who are also assignable persons. It seems to me that this feature in the case—a right in some person, correlative to the moral obligation—constitutes the specific difference between justice, and generosity or beneficence. Justice implies something which it is not only right to do, and wrong not to do, but which some individual person can claim from us as his moral right. No one has a moral right to our generosity or beneficence, because we are not morally bound to practice those virtues towards any given individual. And it will be found with respect to this, as to every correct definition, that the instances which seem to conflict with it are those which most confirm it. For if a moralist attempts, as some have done, to make

---

1 [Mill's note:] See this point enforced and illustrated by Professor [Alexander] Bain [1818–1903], in an admirable chapter (entitled "the Ethical Emotions, or the Moral Sense"), of the second of the two treatises composing his elaborate and profound work on the Mind [*The Emotions and the Will* (London: Parker, 1859)].

out that mankind generally, though not any given individual, have a right to all the good we can do them, he at once, by that thesis, includes generosity and beneficence within the category of justice. He is obliged to say, that our utmost exertions are *due* to our fellow creatures, thus assimilating them to a debt; or that nothing less can be a sufficient *return* for what society does for us, thus classing the case as one of gratitude; both of which are acknowledged cases of justice. Wherever there is right, the case is one of justice, and not of the virtue of beneficence: and whoever does not place the distinction between justice and morality in general, where we have now placed it, will be found to make no distinction between them at all, but to merge all morality in justice.

∞

Having thus endeavored to determine the distinctive elements which enter into the composition of the idea of justice, we are ready to enter on the inquiry, whether the feeling, which accompanies the idea, is attached to it by a special dispensation of nature, or whether it could have grown up, by any known laws, out of the idea itself; and in particular, whether it can have originated in considerations of general expediency.

I conceive that the sentiment itself does not arise from anything which would commonly, or correctly, be termed an idea of expediency; but that though the sentiment does not, whatever is moral in it does.

We have seen that the two essential ingredients in the sentiment of justice are, the desire to punish a person who has done harm, and the knowledge or belief that there is some definite individual or individuals to whom harm has been done.

Now it appears to me, that the desire to punish a person who has done harm to some individual is a spontaneous outgrowth from two sentiments, both in the highest degree natural, and which either are or resemble instincts; the impulse of self-defense, and the feeling of sympathy.

It is natural to resent, and to repel or retaliate, any harm done or attempted against ourselves, or against those with whom we sympathize. The origin of this sentiment it is not necessary here to discuss. Whether it be an instinct or a result of intelligence, it is, we know, common to all animal nature; for every animal tries to hurt those who have hurt, or who it thinks are about to hurt, itself or its young. Human beings, on this point, only differ from other animals in two particulars. First, in being capable of sympathizing, not solely with their offspring, or, like some of the more noble animals, with some superior animal who is kind to them, but with all human, and even with all sentient, beings. Secondly, in having a more developed intelligence, which gives a wider range to the whole of their sentiments, whether self-regarding or sympathetic. By virtue of his superior intelligence, even apart from his superior range of sympathy, a human being is capable of apprehending a community of interest between himself and the human society of which he forms a part, such that any conduct which threatens the security of the society generally, is threatening to his own, and calls forth his instinct (if instinct it be) of self-defense. The same superiority of intelligence joined to the power of sympathizing with human beings generally, enables him to attach himself to the collective idea of his tribe, his country, or mankind, in such a manner that any act hurtful to them, raises his instinct of sympathy, and urges him to resistance.

The sentiment of justice, in that one of its elements which consists of the desire to punish, is thus, I conceive, the natural feeling of retaliation or vengeance, rendered by intellect and sympathy applicable to those injuries, that is, to those hurts, which wound us through, or in common with, society at large. This sentiment, in itself, has nothing moral in it; what is moral is, the exclusive subordination of it to the social sympathies, so as to wait on and obey their call. For the natural feeling would make us resent indiscriminately whatever any one does that is disagreeable to us; but when moralized by the social feeling, it only acts in the directions conformable to the general good: just persons resenting a hurt to society, though not otherwise a hurt to themselves, and not resenting a hurt to themselves, however painful, unless it be of the kind which society has a common interest with them in the repression of.

It is no objection against this doctrine to say, that when we feel our sentiment of justice outraged, we are not thinking of society at large, or of any collective interest, but only of the individual case. It is common enough certainly, though the reverse of commendable, to feel resentment merely because we have suffered pain; but a person whose resentment is really a moral feeling, that is, who considers whether an act is blamable before he allows himself to resent it—such a person, though he may not say expressly to himself that he is standing up for the interest of society, certainly does feel that he is asserting a rule which is for the benefit of others as well as for his own. If he is not feeling this—if he is regarding the act solely as it affects him individually—he is not consciously just; he is not concerning himself about the justice of his actions. This is admitted even by anti-utilitarian moralists. When Kant (as before remarked) propounds as the fundamental principle of morals, "So act, that thy rule of conduct might be adopted as a law by all rational beings," he virtually acknowledges that the interest of mankind collectively, or at least of mankind indiscriminately, must be in the mind of the agent when conscientiously deciding on the morality of the act. Otherwise he uses words without a meaning: for, that a rule even of utter selfishness could not possibly be adopted by all rational beings—that there is any insuperable obstacle in the nature of things to its adoption—cannot be even plausibly maintained. To give any meaning to Kant's principle, the sense put upon it must be, that we ought to shape our conduct by a rule which all rational beings might adopt *with benefit to their collective interest.*

To recapitulate: the idea of justice supposes two things; a rule of conduct, and a sentiment which sanctions the rule. The first must be supposed common to all mankind, and intended for their good. The other (the sentiment) is a desire that punishment may be suffered by those who infringe the rule. There is involved, in addition, the conception of some definite person who suffers by the infringement; whose rights (to use the expression appropriated to the case) are violated by it. And the sentiment of justice appears to me to be, the animal desire to repel or retaliate a hurt or damage to oneself, or to those with whom one sympathizes, widened so as to include all persons, by the human capacity of enlarged sympathy, and the human conception of intelligent self-interest. From the latter elements, the feeling derives its morality; from the former, its peculiar impressiveness, and energy of self-assertion.

I have, throughout, treated the idea of a *right* residing in the injured person, and violated by the injury, not as a separate element in the composition of the idea and sentiment, but as one of the forms in which the other two elements clothe themselves. These elements are, a hurt to some assignable person or persons on the one hand, and a demand for punishment on the other. An examination of our own minds, I think, will show, that these two things include all that we mean when we speak of violation of a right. When we call anything a person's right, we mean that he has a valid claim on society to protect him in the possession of it, either by the force of law, or by that of education and opinion. If he has what we consider a sufficient claim, on whatever account, to have something guaranteed to him by society, we say that he has a right to it. If we desire to prove that anything does not belong to him by right, we think this done as soon as it is admitted that society ought not to take measures for securing it to him, but should leave him to chance, or to his own exertions. Thus, a person is said to have a right to what he can earn in fair professional competition; because society ought not to allow any other person to hinder him from endeavoring to earn in that manner as much as he can. But he has not a right to three hundred a-year, though he may happen to be earning it; because society is not called on to provide that he shall earn that sum. On the contrary, if he owns ten thousand pounds three per cent stock, he *has* a right to three hundred a-year; because society has come under an obligation to provide him with an income of that amount.

To have a right, then, is, I conceive, to have something which society ought to defend me in the possession of. If the objector goes on to ask, why it ought? I can give him no other reason than general utility. If that expression does not seem to convey a sufficient feeling of the strength of the obligation, nor to account for the peculiar energy of the feeling, it is because there goes to the composition of the sentiment, not a rational only, but also an animal element, the thirst for retaliation; and this thirst derives its intensity, as well as its moral justification, from the extraordinarily important and impressive kind of utility which is concerned. The interest involved is that of security, to every one's feelings the most vital of all interests. Nearly all other earthly benefits are needed by one person, not needed by another; and many of them can, if necessary, be cheerfully foregone, or replaced by something else; but security no human being can possibly do without; on it we depend for all our immunity from evil, and for the whole value of all and every good, beyond the passing moment; since nothing but the gratification of the instant could be of any worth to us, if we could be deprived of anything the next instant by whoever was momentarily stronger than ourselves. Now this most indispensable of all necessaries, after physical nutriment, cannot be had, unless the machinery for providing it is kept unintermittedly in active play. Our notion, therefore, of the claim we have on our fellow-creatures to join in making safe for us the very groundwork of our existence, gathers feelings around it so much more intense than those concerned in any of the more common cases of utility, that the difference in degree (as is often the case in psychology) becomes a real difference in kind. The claim assumes that character of absoluteness, that apparent infinity, and incommensurability with all other considerations, which constitute the distinction between the feeling of right and wrong and that of ordinary expediency and inexpediency. The feelings concerned are so powerful, and we count so positively on finding a responsive feeling in others (all being alike interested), that *ought* and *should* grow into *must*, and recognised indispensability becomes a moral necessity, analogous to physical, and often not inferior to it in binding force.

∞

If the preceding analysis, or something resembling it, be not the correct account of the notion of justice; if justice be totally independent of utility, and be a standard *per se*, which the mind can recognise by simple introspection of itself; it is hard to understand why that internal oracle is so ambiguous, and why so many things appear either just or unjust, according to the light in which they are regarded.

We are continually informed that Utility is an uncertain standard, which every different person interprets differently, and that there is no safety but in the immutable, ineffaceable, and unmistakable dictates of Justice, which carry their evidence in themselves, and are independent of the fluctuations of opinion. One would suppose from this that on questions of justice there could be no controversy; that if we take that for our rule, its application to any given case could leave us in as little doubt as a mathematical demonstration. So far is this from being the fact, that there is as much difference of opinion, and as fierce discussion, about what is just, as about what is useful to society. Not only have different nations and individuals different notions of justice, but in the mind of one and the same individual, justice is not some one rule, principle, or maxim, but many, which do not always coincide in their dictates, and in choosing between which, he is guided either by some extraneous standard, or by his own personal predilections.

For instance, there are some who say, that it is unjust to punish any one for the sake of example to others; that punishment is just, only when intended for the good of the sufferer himself. Others maintain the extreme reverse, contending that to punish persons who have attained years of discretion, for their own benefit, is despotism and injustice, since if the matter at issue is solely their own good, no one has a right to control their own judgment of it; but that they may justly be punished to prevent evil to others, this being the exercise of the legitimate right of self-defence. Mr Owen,[1] again, affirms that it is unjust to punish at all; for the criminal did not make his own character; his education, and the circumstances which surrounded him, have made him a criminal, and for these he is not responsible. All these opinions are extremely plausible; and so long as the question is argued as one of justice simply, without going down to the principles which lie under justice and are the source of its authority, I am unable to see how any of these reasoners can be refuted. For in truth every one of the three builds upon rules of justice confessedly true. The first ap-

---

1   Robert Owen (1771–1858), was a Welsh industrialist and social reformer who established a model industrial community at New Lanark, Scotland.

peals to the acknowledged injustice of singling out an individual, and making him a sacrifice, without his consent, for other people's benefit. The second relies on the acknowledged justice of self-defence, and the admitted injustice of forcing one person to conform to another's notions of what constitutes his good. The Owenite invokes the admitted principle, that it is unjust to punish any one for what he cannot help. Each is triumphant so long as he is not compelled to take into consideration any other maxims of justice than the one he has selected; but as soon as their several maxims are brought face to face, each disputant seems to have exactly as much to say for himself as the others. No one of them can carry out his own notion of justice without trampling upon another equally binding. These are difficulties; they have always been felt to be such; and many devices have been invented to turn rather than to overcome them. As a refuge from the last of the three, men imagined what they called the freedom of the will; fancying that they could not justify punishing a man whose will is in a thoroughly hateful state, unless it be supposed to have come into that state through no influence of anterior circumstances. To escape from the other difficulties, a favourite contrivance has been the fiction of a contract, whereby at some unknown period all the members of society engaged to obey the laws, and consented to be punished for any disobedience to them; thereby giving to their legislators the right, which it is assumed they would not otherwise have had, of punishing them, either for their own good or for that of society. This happy thought was considered to get rid of the whole difficulty, and to legitimate the infliction of punishment, in virtue of another received maxim of justice, *volenti non fit injuria*;[1] that is not unjust which is done with the consent of the person who is supposed to be hurt by it. I need hardly remark, that even if the consent were not a mere fiction, this maxim is not superior in authority to the others which it is brought in to supersede. It is, on the contrary, an instructive specimen of the loose and irregular manner in which supposed principles of justice grow up. This particular one evidently came into use as a help to the coarse exigencies of courts of law, which are sometimes obliged to be content with very uncertain presumptions, on account of the greater evils which would often arise from any attempt on their part to cut finer. But even courts of law are not able to adhere consistently to the maxim, for they allow voluntary engagements to be set aside on the ground of fraud, and sometimes on that of mere mistake or misinformation.

---

1   Latin: "To one who is willing, no injury is done."

Again, when the legitimacy of inflicting punishment is admitted, how many conflicting conceptions of justice come to light in discussing the proper apportionment of punishments to offences. No rule on the subject recommends itself so strongly to the primitive and spontaneous sentiment of justice, as the *lex talionis*,[1] an eye for an eye and a tooth for a tooth. Though this principle of the Jewish and of the Mahomedan[2] law has been generally abandoned in Europe as a practical maxim, there is, I suspect, in most minds, a secret hankering after it; and when retribution accidentally falls on an offender in that precise shape, the general feeling of satisfaction evinced bears witness how natural is the sentiment to which this repayment in kind is acceptable. With many, the test of justice in penal infliction is that the punishment should be proportioned to the offence; meaning that it should be exactly measured by the moral guilt of the culprit (whatever be their standard for measuring moral guilt): the consideration, what amount of punishment is necessary to deter from the offence, having nothing to do with the question of justice, in their estimation: while there are others to whom that consideration is all in all; who maintain that it is not just, at least for man, to inflict on a fellow-creature, whatever may be his offences, any amount of suffering beyond the least that will suffice to prevent him from repeating, and others from imitating, his misconduct.

To take another example from a subject already once referred to. In a co-operative industrial association, is it just or not that talent or skill should give a title to superior remuneration? On the negative side of the question it is argued, that whoever does the best he can, deserves equally well, and ought not in justice to be put in a position of inferiority for no fault of his own; that superior abilities have already advantages more than enough, in the admiration they excite, the personal influence they command, and the internal sources of satisfaction attending them, without adding to these a superior share of the world's goods; and that society is bound in justice rather to make compensation to the less favoured, for this unmerited inequality of advantages, than to aggravate it. On the contrary side it is contended, that society receives more from the more efficient labourer; that his services being more useful, society owes him a larger return for them; that a greater

---

1   Latin: The "law of retaliation"; the principle that when one person wrongly injures another the injurer ought to be punished with the same injury (whether physical, monetary, or other).

2   Muslim; the term "Mahomedan," while common in Mill's time, is today considered a misnomer.

share of the joint result is actually his work, and not to allow his claim to it is a kind of robbery; that if he is only to receive as much as others, he can only be justly required to produce as much, and to give a smaller amount of time and exertion, proportioned to his superior efficiency. Who shall decide between these appeals to conflicting principles of justice? Justice has in this case two sides to it, which it is impossible to bring into harmony, and the two disputants have chosen opposite sides; the one looks to what it is just that the individual should receive, the other to what it is just that the community should give. Each, from his own point of view, is unanswerable; and any choice between them, on grounds of justice, must be perfectly arbitrary. Social utility alone can decide the preference.

How many, again, and how irreconcilable, are the standards of justice to which reference is made in discussing the repartition of taxation. One opinion is, that payment to the State should be in numerical proportion to pecuniary means. Others think that justice dictates what they term graduated taxation; taking a higher percentage from those who have more to spare. In point of natural justice a strong case might be made for disregarding means altogether, and taking the same absolute sum (whenever it could be got) from every one: as the subscribers to a mess, or to a club, all pay the same sum for the same privileges, whether they can all equally afford it or not. Since the protection (it might be said) of law and government is afforded to, and is equally required by all, there is no injustice in making all buy it at the same price. It is reckoned justice, not injustice, that a dealer should charge to all customers the same price for the same article, not a price varying according to their means of payment. This doctrine, as applied to taxation, finds no advocates, because it conflicts so strongly with men's feelings of humanity and perceptions of social expediency; but the principle of justice which it invokes is as true and as binding as those which can be appealed to against it. Accordingly it exerts a tacit influence on the line of defence employed for other modes of assessing taxation. People feel obliged to argue that the State does more for the rich than for the poor, as a justification for its taking more from them: though this is in reality not true, for the rich would be far better able to protect themselves, in the absence of law or government, than the poor, and indeed would probably be successful in converting the poor into their slaves. Others, again, so far defer to the same conception of justice, as to maintain that all should pay an equal capitation tax for the protection of their persons (these being of equal value to all), and an unequal tax for the protection of their property, which is unequal. To this others reply, that the all of one man is as valuable to him as the all of another. From these confusions there is no other mode of extrication than the utilitarian.

∞

Is, then, the difference between the Just and the Expedient a merely imaginary distinction? Have mankind been under a delusion in thinking that justice is a more sacred thing than policy, and that the latter ought only to be listened to after the former has been satisfied? By no means. The exposition we have given of the nature and origin of the sentiment, recognises a real distinction; and no one of those who profess the most sublime contempt for the consequences of actions as an element in their morality, attaches more importance to the distinction than I do. While I dispute the pretensions of any theory which sets up an imaginary standard of justice not grounded on utility, I account the justice which is grounded on utility to be the chief part, and incomparably the most sacred and binding part, of all morality. Justice is a name for certain classes of moral rules, which concern the essentials of human well-being more nearly, and are therefore of more absolute obligation, than any other rules for the guidance of life; and the notion which we have found to be of the essence of the idea of justice, that of a right residing in an individual, implies and testifies to this more binding obligation.

The moral rules which forbid mankind to hurt one another (in which we must never forget to include wrongful interference with each other's freedom) are more vital to human well-being than any maxims, however important, which only point out the best mode of managing some department of human affairs. They have also the peculiarity, that they are the main element in determining the whole of the social feelings of mankind. It is their observance which alone preserves peace among human beings: if obedience to them were not the rule, and disobedience the exception, every one would see in every one else a probable enemy, against whom he must be perpetually guarding himself. What is hardly less important, these are the precepts which mankind have the strongest and the most direct inducements for impressing upon one another. By merely giving to each other prudential instruction or exhortation, they may gain, or think they gain, nothing: in inculcating on each other the duty of positive beneficence they have an unmistakable interest, but far less in degree: a person may possibly not need the benefits of others; but he always needs that they should not do him hurt. Thus the moralities which protect every individual from being harmed by others, either directly or by being hindered in his freedom of pursuing his own good, are at once those which he himself has most at heart, and those which he has the strongest interest in publishing and enforcing by word and deed. It is by a person's observance of these that his fitness to exist as one of the fellowship of human beings is tested and decided; for on that depends his being a nuisance or not to those with whom he is in contact. Now it is these moralities primarily which compose the obligations of justice. The most marked cases of injustice, and those which give the tone to the feeling of repugnance which characterises the sentiment, are acts of wrongful aggression, or wrongful exercise of power over some one; the next are those which consist in wrongfully withholding from him something which is his due; in both cases, inflicting on him a positive hurt, either in the form of direct suffering, or of the privation of some good which he had reasonable ground, either of a physical or of a social kind, for counting upon.

The same powerful motives which command the observance of these primary moralities, enjoin the punishment of those who violate them; and as the impulses of self-defence, of defence of others, and of vengeance, are all called forth against such persons, retribution, or evil for evil, becomes closely connected with the sentiment of justice, and is universally included in the idea. Good for good is also one of the dictates of justice; and this, though its social utility is evident, and though it carries with it a natural human feeling, has not at first sight that obvious connection with hurt or injury, which, existing in the most elementary cases of just and unjust, is the source of the characteristic intensity of the sentiment. But the connection, though less obvious, is not less real. He who accepts benefits, and denies a return of them when needed, inflicts a real hurt, by disappointing one of the most natural and reasonable of expectations, and one which he must at least tacitly have encouraged, otherwise the benefits would seldom have been conferred. The important rank, among human evils and wrongs, of the disappointment of expectation, is shown in the fact that it constitutes the principal criminality of two such highly immoral acts as a breach of friendship and a breach of promise. Few hurts which human beings can sustain are greater, and none wound more, than when that on which they habitually and with full assurance relied, fails them in the hour of need; and few wrongs are greater than this mere withholding of good; none excite more resentment, either in the person suffering, or in a sympathising spectator. The principle, therefore, of giving to each what they deserve, that is, good for good as well as evil for evil, is not only included within the idea of Justice as we have defined it, but is a proper object of that intensity of sentiment, which places the Just, in human estimation, above the simply Expedient.

Most of the maxims of justice current in the world, and commonly appealed to in its transactions, are simply instrumental to carrying into effect the principles of justice which we have now spoken of. That a person is only responsible for what he has done voluntarily, or could voluntarily have avoided; that it is unjust to condemn any person unheard; that the punishment ought to be proportioned to the offence, and the like, are maxims intended to prevent the just principle of evil for evil from being perverted to the infliction of evil without that justification. The greater part of these common maxims have come into use from the practice of courts of justice, which have been naturally led to a more complete recognition and elaboration than was likely to suggest itself to others, of the rules necessary to enable them to fulfil their double function, of inflicting punishment when due, and of awarding to each person his right.

That first of judicial virtues, impartiality, is an obligation of justice, partly for the reason last mentioned; as being a necessary condition of the fulfilment of the other obligations of justice. But this is not the only source of the exalted rank, among human obligations, of those maxims of equality and impartiality, which, both in popular estimation and in that of the most enlightened, are included among the precepts of justice. In one point of view, they may be considered as corollaries from the principles already laid down. If it is a duty to do to each according to his deserts, returning good for good as well as repressing evil by evil, it necessarily follows that we should treat all equally well (when no higher duty forbids) who have deserved equally well of us, and that society should treat all equally well who have deserved equally well of it, that is, who have deserved equally well absolutely. This is the highest abstract standard of social and distributive justice; towards which all institutions, and the efforts of all virtuous citizens, should be made in the utmost possible degree to converge. But this great moral duty rests upon a still deeper foundation, being a direct emanation from the first principle of morals, and not a mere logical corollary from secondary or derivative doctrines. It is involved in the very meaning of Utility, or the Greatest Happiness Principle. That principle is a mere form of words without rational signification, unless one person's happiness, supposed equal in degree (with the proper allowance made for kind), is counted for exactly as much as another's. Those conditions being supplied, Bentham's dictum, "everybody to count for one, nobody for more than one," might be written under the principle of utility as an explanatory

commentary.[1] The equal claim of everybody to happiness in the estimation of the moralist and the legislator, involves an equal claim to
all the means of happiness, except in so far as the inevitable conditions of human life, and the general interest, in which that of every individual is included, set limits to the maxim; and those limits ought
to be strictly construed. As every other maxim of justice, so this is by
no means applied or held applicable universally; on the contrary, as I
have already remarked, it bends to every person's ideas of social expediency. But in whatever case it is deemed applicable at all, it is held
to be the dictate of justice. All persons are deemed to have a *right* to
equality of treatment, except when some recognised social expediency requires the reverse. And hence all social inequalities which
have ceased to be considered expedient, assume the character not of
simple inexpediency, but of injustice, and appear so tyrannical, that

---

1   [Mill's note:] This implication, in the first principle of the utilitarian scheme, of
perfect impartiality between persons, is regarded by Mr Herbert Spencer (in his
Social Statics) as a disproof of the pretensions of utility to be a sufficient guide to
right; since (he says) the principle of utility presupposes the anterior principle,
that everybody has an equal right to happiness. It may be more correctly described
as supposing that equal amounts of happiness are equally desirable, whether felt
by the same or by different persons. This, however, is not a pre-supposition; not a
premise needful to support the principle of utility, but the very principle itself; for
what is the principle of utility, if it be not that "happiness" and "desirable" are
synonymous terms? If there is any anterior principle implied, it can be no other
than this, that the truths of arithmetic are applicable to the valuation of happiness,
as of all other measurable quantities.

   Mr Herbert Spencer, in a private communication on the subject of the preceding
Note, objects to being considered an opponent of utilitarianism, and states that he
regards happiness as the ultimate end of morality; but deems that end only par-
tially attainable by empirical generalisations from the observed results of conduct,
and completely attainable only by deducing, from the laws of life and the conditions of existence, what kinds of action necessarily tend to produce happiness, and
what kinds to produce unhappiness. With the exception of the word "necessarily,"
I have no dissent to express from this doctrine; and (omitting that word) I am not
aware that any modern advocate of utilitarianism is of a different opinion. Bentham, certainly, to whom in the *Social Statics* Mr Spencer particularly referred, is,
least of all writers, chargeable with unwillingness to deduce the effect of actions
on happiness from the laws of human nature and the universal conditions of
human life. The common charge against him is of relying too exclusively upon
such deductions, and declining altogether to be bound by the generalisations from
specific experience which Mr Spencer thinks that utilitarians generally confine
themselves to. My own opinion (and, as I collect, Mr Spencer's) is, that in ethics,
as in all other branches of scientific study, the consilience of the results of both
these processes, each corroborating and verifying the other, is requisite to give to
any general proposition the kind and degree of evidence which constitutes scientific proof. [Herbert Spencer (1820–1903) was a philosopher and sociologist. *Social Statics* (1851) was his first book.]

people are apt to wonder how they ever could have been tolerated; forgetful that they themselves perhaps tolerate other inequalities under an equally mistaken notion of expediency, the correction of which would make that which they approve seem quite as monstrous as what they have at last learnt to condemn. The entire history of social improvement has been a series of transitions, by which one custom or institution after another, from being a supposed primary necessity of social existence, has passed into the rank of a universally stigmatised injustice and tyranny. So it has been with the distinctions of slaves and freemen, nobles and serfs, patricians and plebeians; and so it will be, and in part already is, with the aristocracies of colour, race, and sex.

It appears from what has been said, that justice is a name for certain moral requirements, which, regarded collectively, stand higher in the scale of social utility, and are therefore of more paramount obligation, than any others; though particular cases may occur in which some other social duty is so important, as to overrule any one of the general maxims of justice. Thus, to save a life, it may not only be allowable, but a duty, to steal, or take by force, the necessary food or medicine, or to kidnap, and compel to officiate, the only qualified medical practitioner. In such cases, as we do not call anything justice which is not a virtue, we usually say, not that justice must give way to some other moral principle, but that what is just in ordinary cases is, by reason of that other principle, not just in the particular case. By this useful accommodation of language, the character of indefeasibility[1] attributed to justice is kept up, and we are saved from the necessity of maintaining that there can be laudable injustice.

The considerations which have now been adduced resolve, I conceive, the only real difficulty in the utilitarian theory of morals. It has always been evident that all cases of justice are also cases of expediency: the difference is in the peculiar sentiment which attaches to the former, as contradistinguished from the latter. If this characteristic sentiment has been sufficiently accounted for; if there is no necessity to assume for it any peculiarity of origin; if it is simply the natural feeling of resentment, moralized by being made coextensive with the demands of social good; and if this feeling not only does but ought to exist in all the classes of cases to which the idea of justice corresponds; that idea no longer presents itself as a stumbling-block to the utilitarian ethics. Justice remains the appropriate name for certain social utilities which are vastly more important, and therefore more absolute and imperative, than any others are as a class (though not more so than

---

1   Inability to be annulled or made inapplicable.

others may be in particular cases); and which, therefore, ought to be, as well as naturally are, guarded by a sentiment not only different in degree, but also in kind; distinguished from the milder feeling which attaches to the mere idea of promoting human pleasure or convenience, at once by the more definite nature of its commands, and by the sterner character of its sanctions.

Appendix:
from Jeremy Bentham's *An Introduction to the Principles of Morals and Legislation*

Who Was Jeremy Bentham?

Jeremy Bentham (1748–1832) is generally regarded as the first modern Western philosopher to give utilitarian ideas a central place in his thought. He discusses the "principle of utility" at length in both of his best known works, *A Fragment on Government* (1776) and *An Introduction to the Principles of Morals and Legislation* (1789). Bentham's ideas were central to the education of John Stuart Mill, whose father James Mill served as Bentham's secretary.

Bentham was born in 1748 in London, England. His father was a wealthy, well-educated, politically ambitious lawyer who wanted to ensure that Jeremy, his eldest son, was well prepared for economic and political success in life. Bentham began to read Latin at age three and attended the prestigious Westminster School before being sent to Oxford at age twelve. He received a Bachelor's degree at age fifteen. As his father and grandfather had done, he then studied law, passing the bar in 1769 at age twenty-one. Despite his father's hopes that he would then begin a successful legal career, Bentham decided that he wanted to devote his career to further academic study aimed at finding ways to reform public institutions.

In 1768 Bentham read Joseph Priestley's (1733–1804) just-published *The First Principles of Government*. Priestley's ideas—and in particular his use of the phrase "the greatest happiness for the greatest number"—greatly influenced Bentham in his first formulations of utilitarian ideas in *A Fragment on Government*. He argued, for example, that an assessment of the quality of a legal system should be based on how it contributes to the overall happiness of the members of society.

Bentham's first interest was reform of the penal system. He argued that rehabilitation, not punishment, should be the central feature of the system. Bentham's first book, *A Fragment on Government*, critiqued the writings of William Blackstone (1723–80), the most prominent English legal scholar at the time.

By 1780, Bentham had finished writing *An Introduction to the Principles of Morals and Legislation* (though the book was not actually published until 1789). In this work he elaborates and extends his

utilitarian arguments to cover all areas of moral philosophy, proposing a "felicific calculus" for evaluating pleasures and pains in terms
of intensity, duration, certainty, propinquity (closeness), fecundity (or
how likely it is to be followed by sensations of the same kind), purity,
and extent (i.e., the number of people affected). Since Bentham saw
human motivation as rooted in seeking pleasures and avoiding pains,
the best political and legal systems would help citizens to achieve
those goals.

During the last half of Bentham's life he was an extremely active
writer, but much of his output was never published in his lifetime. He
left voluminous manuscripts, some of which were not published until
more than a century after his death. His later writings include a more
comprehensive version of his *A Fragment on Government* and work on
such varied topics as the relationship between the state and religious
institutions, political equality for women, slavery, animal rights, opposition to corporal punishment, and support for tolerance of homo-
sexuality (in the essay "Offences Against One's Self"); on many of
these subjects Bentham's views were far ahead of his time.

In 1828, University College London was founded, in large part as
a result of Bentham's advocacy of an expansion of educational opportunities. Upon his death in 1832, Bentham's will stipulated that his
body was to be preserved and placed on display at the college. His
"auto-icon," as it is called, can still be found there to this day. The College has also honored Bentham's legacy in more traditional ways:
since 1968 it has been working on a project to publish all of Bentham's
writings in a single collection. To date, 32 of the 70 projected volumes
have been published.

An Introduction to the Principles of Morals and Legislation (1780; published 1789)

Chapter 1: Of the Principle of Utility

I. Nature has placed mankind under the governance of two sovereign
masters, *pain* and *pleasure*. It is for them alone to point out what we
ought to do, as well as to determine what we shall do. On the one hand
the standard of right and wrong, on the other the chain of causes and
effects, are fastened to their throne. They govern us in all we do, in all
we say, in all we think: every effort we can make to throw off our subjection, will serve but to demonstrate and confirm it. In words a man
may pretend to abjure their empire: but in reality he will remain sub-

ject to it all the while. The *principle of utility*[1] recognizes this subjection, and assumes it for the foundation of that system, the object of which is to rear the fabric of felicity by the hands of reason and of law. Systems which attempt to question it, deal in sounds instead of sense, in caprice instead of reason, in darkness instead of light.

But enough of metaphor and declamation: it is not by such means that moral science is to be improved.

II. The principle of utility is the foundation of the present work: it will be proper therefore at the outset to give an explicit and determinate account of what is meant by it. By the principle[2] of utility is meant that principle which approves or disapproves of every action whatsoever, according to the tendency it appears to have to augment or diminish the happiness of the party whose interest is in question: or, what is the same thing in other words, to promote or to oppose that happiness. I say of every action whatsoever, and therefore not only of every action of a private individual, but of every measure of government.

---

1   [Bentham's note:] To this denomination has of late been added, or substituted, the *greatest happiness* or *greatest felicity* principle: this for shortness, instead of saying at length that principle which states the greatest happiness of all those whose interest is in question, as being the right and proper, and only right and proper and universally desirable, end of human action: of human action in every situation, and in particular in that of a functionary [i.e., *official*] or set of functionaries exercising the powers of Government. The word *utility* does not so clearly point to the ideas of *pleasure* and *pain* as the words *happiness* and *felicity* do: nor does it lead us to the consideration of the *number*, of the interests affected; to the *number*, as being the circumstance, which contributes, in the largest proportion, to the formation of the standard here in question; the *standard of right and wrong*, by which alone the propriety of human conduct, in every situation, can with propriety be tried [i.e., *determined*]. This want [i.e., *lack*] of a sufficiently manifest connection between the ideas of *happiness* and *pleasure* on the one hand, and the idea of *utility* on the other, I have every now and then found operating, and with but too much efficiency, as a bar to the acceptance, that might otherwise have been given, to this principle.

2   [Bentham's note:] The word *principle* is derived from the Latin *principium*: which seems to be compounded of the two words *primus*, first, or chief, and *cipium*, a termination which seems to be derived from *capio*, to take, as in *mancipium*, *municipium*; to which are analogous, *auceps*, *forceps*, and others. It is a term of very vague and very extensive signification: it is applied to any thing which is conceived to serve as a foundation or beginning to any series of operations: in some cases, of physical operations; but of mental operations in the present case.

    The principle here in question may be taken for an act of the mind; a sentiment; a sentiment of approbation; a sentiment which, when applied to an action, approves of its utility, as that quality of it by which the measure of approbation or disapprobation bestowed upon it ought to be governed.

III. By utility is meant that property in any object, whereby it tends to produce benefit, advantage, pleasure, good, or happiness, (all this in the present case comes to the same thing) or (what comes again to the same thing) to prevent the happening of mischief, pain, evil, or unhappiness to the party whose interest is considered: if that party be the community in general, then the happiness of the community: if a particular individual, then the happiness of that individual.

IV. The interest of the community is one of the most general expressions that can occur in the phraseology of morals: no wonder that the meaning of it is often lost. When it has a meaning, it is this. The community is a fictitious *body*, composed of the individual persons who are considered as constituting as it were its *members*. The interest of the community then is, what?—the sum of the interests of the several members who compose it.

V. It is in vain to talk of the interest of the community, without understanding what is the interest of the individual. A thing is said to promote the interest, or to be *for* the interest, of an individual, when it tends to add to the sum total of his pleasures: or, what comes to the same thing, to diminish the sum total of his pains.

VI. An action then may be said to be conformable to the principle of utility, or, for shortness sake, to utility, (meaning with respect to the community at large) when the tendency it has to augment the happiness of the community is greater than any it has to diminish it.

VII. A measure of government (which is but a particular kind of action, performed by a particular person or persons) may be said to be conformable to or dictated by the principle of utility, when in like manner the tendency which it has to augment the happiness of the community is greater than any which it has to diminish it.

VIII. When an action, or in particular a measure of government, is supposed by a man to be conformable to the principle of utility, it may be convenient, for the purposes of discourse, to imagine a kind of law or dictate, called a law or dictate[1] of utility: and to speak of the action in question, as being conformable to such law or dictate.

IX. A man may be said to be a partisan of the principle of utility, when the approbation or disapprobation he annexes to any action, or to any

---

1   Command, guiding principle.

measure, is determined by and proportioned to the tendency which he conceives it to have to augment or to diminish the happiness of the community: or in other words, to its conformity or unconformity to the laws or dictates of utility.

X. Of an action that is conformable to the principle of utility one may always say either that it is one that ought to be done, or at least that it is not one that ought not to be done. One may say also, that it is right it should be done; at least that it is not wrong it should be done: that it is a right action; at least that it is not a wrong action. When thus interpreted, the words *ought*, and *right* and *wrong* and others of that stamp, have a meaning: when otherwise, they have none.

XI. Has the rectitude of this principle been ever formally contested? It should seem that it had, by those who have not known what they have been meaning. Is it susceptible of any direct proof? it should seem not: for that which is used to prove everything else, cannot itself be proved: a chain of proofs must have their commencement somewhere. To give such proof is as impossible as it is needless.

XII. Not that there is or ever has been that human creature at breathing, however stupid or perverse, who has not on many, perhaps on most occasions of his life, deferred to it. By the natural constitution of the human frame, on most occasions of their lives men in general embrace this principle, without thinking of it: if not for the ordering of their own actions, yet for the trying of their own actions, as well as of those of other men. There have been, at the same time, not many perhaps, even of the most intelligent, who have been disposed to embrace it purely and without reserve. There are even few who have not taken some occasion or other to quarrel with it, either on account of their not understanding always how to apply it, or on account of some prejudice or other which they were afraid to examine into, or could not bear to part with. For such is the stuff that man is made of: in principle and in practice, in a right track and in a wrong one, the rarest of all human qualities is consistency.

XIII. When a man attempts to combat the principle of utility, it is with reasons drawn, without his being aware of it, from that very principle itself. His arguments, if they prove any thing, prove not that the principle is *wrong*, but that, according to the applications he supposes to be made of it, it is *misapplied*. Is it possible for a man to move the earth? Yes; but he must first find out another earth to stand upon.

XIV. To disprove the propriety of it by arguments is impossible; but, from the causes that have been mentioned, or from some confused or partial view of it, a man may happen to be disposed not to relish it. Where this is the case, if he thinks the settling of his opinions on such a subject worth the trouble, let him take the following steps, and at length, perhaps, he may come to reconcile himself to it.

1. Let him settle with himself, whether he would wish to discard this principle altogether; if so, let him consider what it is that all his reasonings (in matters of politics especially) can amount to?

2. If he would, let him settle with himself, whether he would judge and act without any principle, or whether there is any other he would judge an act by?

3. If there be, let him examine and satisfy himself whether the principle he thinks he has found is really any separate intelligible principle; or whether it be not a mere principle in words, a kind of phrase, which at bottom expresses neither more nor less than the mere averment[1] of his own unfounded sentiments;[2] that is, what in another person he might be apt to call caprice?

4. If he is inclined to think that his own approbation or disapprobation, annexed to the idea of an act, without any regard to its consequences, is a sufficient foundation for him to judge and act upon, let him ask himself whether his sentiment is to be a standard of right and wrong, with respect to every other man, or whether every man's sentiment has the same privilege of being a standard to itself?

5. In the first case, let him ask himself whether his principle is not despotical, and hostile to all the rest of human race?

6. In the second case, whether it is not anarchial, and whether at this rate there are not as many different standards of right and wrong as there are men? and whether even to the same man, the same thing, which is right today, may not (without the least change in its nature) be wrong tomorrow? and whether the same thing is not right and wrong in the same place at the same time? and in either case, whether all argument is not at an end? and whether, when two men have said, "I like this," and "I don't like it," they can (upon such a principle) have any thing more to say?

7. If he should have said to himself, No: for that the sentiment which he proposes as a standard must be grounded on reflection, let him say on what particulars the reflection is to turn? if on particulars having relation to the utility of the act, then let him say whether

---

1 Declaration.
2 Feelings of approval or disapproval.

this is not deserting his own principle, and borrowing assistance from that very one in opposition to which he sets it up: or if not on those particulars, on what other particulars?

8. If he should be for compounding the matter, and adopting his own principle in part, and the principle of utility in part, let him say how far he will adopt it?

9. When he has settled with himself where he will stop, then let him ask himself how he justifies to himself the adopting it so far? and why he will not adopt it any farther?

10. Admitting any other principle than the principle of utility to be a right principle, a principle that it is right for a man to pursue; admitting (what is not true) that the word *right* can have a meaning without reference to utility, let him say whether there is any such thing as a *motive* that a man can have to pursue the dictates of it: if there is, let him say what that motive is, and how it is to be distinguished from those which enforce the dictates of utility: if not, then lastly let him say what it is this other principle can be good for?

Chapter 4: Value of a Lot of Pleasure or Pain, How to Be Measured

I. Pleasures then, and the avoidance of pains, are the *ends* that the legislator has in view; it behooves him therefore to understand their *value*. Pleasures and pains are the *instruments* he has to work with: it behooves him therefore to understand their force, which is again, in other words, their value.

II. To a person considered by *himself*, the value of a pleasure or pain considered *by itself*, will be greater or less, according to the four following *circumstances*:[1]

---

1   [Bentham's note:] These circumstances have since been denominated *elements* or *dimensions* of *value* in a pleasure or a pain.

   Not long after the publication of the first edition, the following memoriter [i.e, connected with memorizing] verses were framed, in the view of lodging more effectually, in the memory, these points, on which the whole fabric of morals and legislation may be seen to rest.

   Intense, long, certain, speedy, fruitful, pure—
   Such marks in *pleasures* and in *pains* endure.
   Such pleasures seek if *private* be thy end:
   If it be *public*, wide let them *extend*
   Such *pains* avoid, whichever be thy view:
   If pains *must* come, let them *extend* to few.

1. Its *intensity*.
2. Its *duration*.
3. Its *certainty* or *uncertainty*.
4. Its *propinquity*[1] or *remoteness*.

III. These are the circumstances which are to be considered in estimating a pleasure or a pain considered each of them by itself. But when
the value of any pleasure or pain is considered for the purpose of estimating the tendency of any act by which it is produced, there are two
other circumstances to be taken into the account; these are,

5. Its *fecundity*, or the chance it has of being followed by sensations
   of the *same* kind: that is, pleasures, if it be a pleasure: pains, if it
   be a pain.
6. Its *purity*, or the chance it has of not being followed by sensations
   of the *opposite* kind: that is, pains, if it be a pleasure: pleasures, if
   it be a pain.

These two last, however, are in strictness scarcely to be deemed properties of the pleasure or the pain itself; they are not, therefore, in strictness to be taken into the account of the value of that pleasure or that
pain. They are in strictness to be deemed properties only of the act, or
other event, by which such pleasure or pain has been produced; and accordingly are only to be taken into the account of the tendency of such
act or such event.

IV. To a *number* of persons, with reference to each of whom to the
value of a pleasure or a pain is considered, it will be greater or less, according to seven circumstances: to wit, the six preceding ones; viz.

1. Its *intensity*.
2. Its *duration*.
3. Its *certainty* or *uncertainty*.
4. Its *propinquity* or *remoteness*.
5. Its *fecundity*.
6. Its *purity*.

And one other; to wit:

7. Its *extent*; that is, the number of persons to whom it *extends*; or (in
   other words) who are affected by it.

V. To take an exact account then of the general tendency of any act, by
which the interests of a community are affected, proceed as follows.
Begin with any one person of those whose interests seem most immediately to be affected by it: and take an account,

---

1 Closeness.

1. Of the value of each distinguishable *pleasure* which appears to be produced by it in the *first* instance.
2. Of the value of each *pain* which appears to be produced by it in the *first* instance.
3. Of the value of each pleasure which appears to be produced by it *after* the first. This constitutes the *fecundity* of the first *pleasure* and the *impurity* of the first *pain*.
4. Of the value of each *pain* which appears to be produced by it after the first. This constitutes the *fecundity* of the first *pain*, and the *impurity* of the first pleasure.
5. Sum up all the values of all the *pleasures* on the one side, and those of all the pains on the other. The balance, if it be on the side of pleasure, will give the *good* tendency of the act upon the whole, with respect to the interests of that *individual* person; if on the side of pain, the *bad* tendency of it upon the whole.
6. Take an account of the *number* of persons whose interests appear to be concerned; and repeat the above process with respect to each. *Sum up* the numbers expressive of the degrees of *good* tendency, which the act has, with respect to each individual, in regard to whom the tendency of it is *good* upon the whole: do this again with respect to each individual, in regard to whom the tendency of it is *good* upon the whole: do this again with respect to each individual, in regard to whom the tendency of it is *bad* upon the whole. Take the *balance* which if on the side of *pleasure*, will give the general *good tendency* of the act, with respect to the total number or community of individuals concerned; if on the side of pain, the general *evil tendency*, with respect to the same community.

VI. It is not to be expected that this process should be strictly pursued previously to every moral judgment, or to every legislative or judicial operation. It may, however, be always kept in view: and as near as the process actually pursued on these occasions approaches to it, so near will such process approach to the character of an exact one.

VII. The same process is alike applicable to pleasure and pain, in whatever shape they appear: and by whatever denomination they are distinguished: to pleasure, whether it be called *good* (which is properly the cause or instrument of pleasure) or *profit* (which is distant pleasure, or the cause or instrument of distant pleasure,) or *convenience*, or *advantage, benefit, emolument*,[1] *happiness*, and so forth: to pain,

---

1 Payment (for work done).

whether it be called *evil*, (which corresponds to *good*) or *mischief*, or *inconvenience*, or *disadvantage*, or *loss*, or *unhappiness*, and so forth.

VIII. Nor is this a novel and unwarranted, any more than it is a useless theory. In all this there is nothing but what the practice of mankind, wheresoever they have a clear view of their own interest, is perfectly conformable to. An article of property, an estate in land, for instance, is valuable, on what account? On account of the pleasures of all kinds which it enables a man to produce, and what comes to the same thing the pains of all kinds which it enables him to avert. But the value of such an article of property is universally understood to rise or fall according to the length or shortness of the time which a man has in it: the certainty or uncertainty of its coming into possession: and the nearness or remoteness of the time at which, if at all, it is to come into possession. As to the *intensity* of the pleasures which a man may derive from it, this is never thought of, because it depends upon the use which each particular person may come to make of it; which cannot be estimated till the particular pleasures he may come to derive from it, or the particular pains he may come to exclude by means of it, are brought to view. For the same reason, neither does he think of the *fecundity* or *purity* of those pleasures.

Thus much for pleasure and pain, happiness and unhappiness, in *general*. We come now to consider the several particular kinds of pain and pleasure.

Index

From the Publisher

A name never says it all, but the word "Broadview" expresses a good deal of the philosophy behind our company. We are open to a broad range of academic approaches and political viewpoints. We pay attention to the broad impact book publishing and book printing has in the wider world; we began using recycled stock more than a decade ago, and for some years now we have used 100% recycled paper for most titles. Our publishing program is internationally oriented and broad-ranging. Our individual titles often appeal to a broad readership too; many are of interest as much to general readers as to academics and students.

Founded in 1985, Broadview remains a fully independent company owned by its shareholders—not an imprint or subsidiary of a larger multinational.

For the most accurate information on our books (including information on pricing, editions, and formats) please visit our website at www.broadviewpress.com. Our print books and ebooks are also available for sale on our site.

On the Broadview website we also offer several goods that are not books—among them the Broadview coffee mug, the Broadview beer stein (inscribed with a line from Geoffrey Chaucer's *Canterbury Tales*), the Broadview fridge magnets (your choice of philosophical or literary), and a range of T-shirts (made from combinations of hemp, bamboo, and/or high-quality pima cotton, with no child labor, sweatshop labor, or environmental degradation involved in their manufacture).

All these goods are available through the "merchandise" section of the Broadview website. When you buy Broadview goods you can support other goods too.

broadview press
www.broadviewpress.com

RECYCLED
Paper made from
recycled material
FSC® C103567

The interior of this book is printed on 100% recycled paper.

PERMANENT

100%

Ancient
Forest
Friendly™